"*Traces of Memory* compellingly reconstruct̶̶̶̶̶̶̶̶̶̶̶̶̶̶ -
able journalist, poet, activist for women's rights and Jewish causes, and a Holocaust
survivor whose literary, journalistic, and testimonial output spans more than half a
century. Sandra Alfers creates a vivid biographical account of this fascinating woman
out of a dispersed archive consisting of published writings, personal correspon-
dence, and family documents. The story she adeptly narrates not only illustrates the
upheavals and ruptures effected by National Socialism and the Holocaust, but also
paints a sociohistorical portrait of the achievements and the disappointments, the
resilience and the fragility of Jewish life in Europe in the first half of the twentieth
century. Presenting for the first time some of Dormitzer's German-language poetry
(particularly poems written during her internment in the Theresienstadt Ghetto) in
Cornelius Partsch's superb translation, *Traces of Memory* rescues from oblivion the
life and work of a singular woman."

— Erin McGlothlin, Professor of German and Jewish
Studies, Washington University in St. Louis

"Stellar scholarship and brilliant writing by Sandra Alfers vividly portray the life and
work of Else Dormitzer, a remarkable Holocaust survivor whose poetry—sensitively
translated from the German by Alfers's partner Cornelius Partsch—merits the atten-
tion that *Traces of Memory* gives it. Alfers and Dormitzer never met, and yet they
interact eloquently in this special book. With deep respect and insight, Alfers ensures
new life for Dormitzer's Holocaust testimony. In turn, Dormitzer helps Alfers to find
her own compelling voice. Witnessing how these two affect each other is sure to cre-
ate a moving and poignant experience for the many readers that *Traces of Memory*
deserves to have."

— John K. Roth, Edward J. Sexton Professor Emeritus of
Philosophy, Claremont McKenna College; Author,
Sources of Holocaust Insight

"Sandra Alfers deserves high praise for bringing the multifaceted life and writing of
Else Dormitzer to the attention of an English-speaking audience in this fine volume.
As an active Jewish community member, journalist, poet, children's book author, and
survivor of *Theresienstadt*, Dormitzer's life is an apt example of German Jewry devas-
tated by the Holocaust. Alfers' expertise as a literary scholar comes to the fore in her
analysis of Dormitzer's poetry written in *Theresienstadt*, available in a new translation
by Cornelius Partsch. The volume is stark evidence for the meaning of art and litera-
ture in the face of utter devastation—and a convincing call for its integration into
historical Holocaust research."

— Dr. Anna Ullrich, European Holocaust
Research Infrastructure (EHRI)

"Through her sharp focus on the life and writing of one woman, Sandra Alfers sheds light on the activities and achievements of German-Jewish women before, during, and after the Holocaust. Beautifully written in clear prose, this volume shows Else Dormitzer's important intellectual and creative contributions as a journalist and political activist, as a poet and witness of Theresienstadt. Insisting on the significance of poetry of the Holocaust, Alfers also expands the canon of Holocaust literature. Together with the rich bilingual appendix that includes Dormitzer's poetry and testimonial accounts, translated by Cornelius Partsch alongside the original German, this Holocaust survivor's works are now accessible to a wider audience."

— Lynn L. Wolff, Associate Professor of German,
Michigan State University

"Sandra Alfers' beautifully written *Traces of Memory: The Life and Work of Else Dormitzer* provides an in-depth study of the life and works of children's book author, journalist, political activist, and Terezín survivor Else Dormitzer. Alfers shows how camp poetry, such as Dormitzer's *Theresienstädter Bilder*, has been marginalized within German academic discourses and she convincingly argues that such texts deserve much more scholarly attention. The book makes available for the first time Dormitzer's original poetry collection from Theresienstadt and three testimonial reports in both the original German and in English—skillfully translated by Cornelius Partsch. Dormitzer's camp poetry and testimonial reports and Alfers' in-depth analysis are must-use texts in Holocaust Studies—for teachers and students alike."

— Natalie Eppelsheimer, Associate Professor
of German, Middlebury College

"Sandra Alfers' book paints a comprehensive and nuanced portrait of the Jewish writer Else Dormitzer, who continued to write in the Theresienstadt ghetto. With impressive analytical clarity, the study gathers and interprets the powerful testimony of this almost forgotten author."

— Saskia Fischer, Leibniz Universität
Hannover, Germany

Traces
of Memory
The Life and Work
of Else Dormitzer
(1877–1958)

The Holocaust:
History and Literature, Ethics and Philosophy

Series Editor
Michael Berenbaum (American Jewish University)

Other Titles in the Series
The Doctors of the Warsaw Ghetto
Maria Ciesielska
Edited by Tali Nates, Jeanette Friedman, and Luc Albinski
With a foreword by Michael Berenbaum
Translated from the original Polish by Agata Krzychylkiewicz

Israel's Failed Response to the Armenian Genocide: Denial, State Deception, Truth versus Politicization of History
Israel W. Charny

Schindler's Listed: The Search for My Father's Lost Gold
Mark Biederman, with Randi Biederman

In Enemy Land: The Jews of Kielce and the Region, 1939–1946
Sara Bender

A Survivor's Duty: Surviving the Holocaust and Fighting for Israel — A Story of Father and Son
Gabriel Laufer

Miracle Child: The Journey of a Young Holocaust Survivor
Anita Epstein with Noel Epstein

Class of '31: A German-Jewish Émigré's Journey across Defeated Germany
Walter Jessel
Edited with an Introduction by Brian E. Crim

Traces of Memory

The Life and Work of Else Dormitzer (1877–1958)

Sandra Alfers
Poetry and testimonial
accounts translated by
Cornelius Partsch

BOSTON
2024

Library of Congress Cataloging-in-Publication Data

Names: Alfers, Sandra, 1971- author. | Partsch, Cornelius, 1967- translator.

Title: Traces of memory: the life and work of Else Dormitzer (1877–1958) / Sandra Alfers; poetry and testimonial accounts translated by Cornelius Partsch.

Other titles: Weiter schreiben. English

Description: Boston: Academic Studies Press, 2024. | Series: The Holocaust: history and literature, ethics and philosophy | Includes bibliographical references.

Identifiers: LCCN 2024002356 (print) | LCCN 2024002357 (ebook) | ISBN 9798887194707 (hardback) | ISBN 9798887194714 (paperback) | ISBN 9798887194721 (adobe pdf) | ISBN 9798887194738 (epub)

Subjects: LCSH: Dormitzer, Else. | Jewish women authors—Germany—20th century—Biography. | Theresienstadt (Concentration camp)—Poetry. | LCGFT: Biographies. | Poetry.

Classification: LCC PT2607.O775 Z5213 2024 (print) | LCC PT2607.O775 (ebook) | DDC 831/.912—dc23/eng/20240122

LC record available at https://lccn.loc.gov/2024002356
LC ebook record available at https://lccn.loc.gov/2024002357

ISBN 9798887194707 (hardback)
ISBN 9798887194714 (paperback)
ISBN 9798887194721 (adobe pdf)
ISBN 9798887194738 (epub)

Book design by Kryon Publishing Services.
Cover design by Ivan Grave.

Published by Academic Studies Press
1577 Beacon Street
Brookline, MA 02446, USA
press@academicstudiespress.com
www.academicstudiespress.com

Meiner Familie

Contents

Acknowledgments

A note of deep gratitude to all who helped bring this book to life. First and foremost, to the surviving relatives of Else Dormitzer in Germany, Luxembourg, the Netherlands, and the United Kingdom: Thomas and Ingrid Runkel, Henk and Liesbeth Haas, Irene Stofkoper-Haas, and George Rogers. They generously opened their homes to me, engaged in frank conversations, and provided answers to my many questions about their family history, be it online or in person. Without their support, the project about their grandmother and great-grandmother would not have come to fruition. Publisher Nora Pester contracted the original German-language version of this book for Hentrich & Hentrich (Leipzig, Germany), where it appeared with patronage from Bernhard Kohlmeier and Lisa Ann Mikulencak (Seattle, WA) as *weiter schreiben. Leben und Lyrik der Else Dormitzer* in 2015. Michael Berenbaum, editor of the special series "The Holocaust: History and Literature, Ethics and Philosophy" for Academic Studies Press (Brookline, MA), and Editorial Director Alessandra Anzani believed in the revised English-language edition from the start, and I thank them and the anonymous peer reviewers for their expertise and guidance in moving the manuscript towards publication. As part of his professional leave granted by Western Washington University (Bellingham, WA), Cornelius Partsch translated Else Dormitzer's three eye-witness accounts and her collection of poetry from German into English, being a trusted and knowledgeable partner along the way. Several individuals and units at Western Washington University supported my research at various times, among them Shannon Dubenion-Smith (chair, Department of Modern and Classical Languages), Paqui Paredes (former dean, College of Humanities and Social Sciences), the Office of Research and Sponsored Programs, the Provost's Office, the Western Foundation, and Western Libraries. The late Stephen Senge (Bellingham, WA) provided additional professional development funds that allowed me to accept an invitation from Anja Ballis (chair, German Language Education) as a visiting research fellow at Ludwig-Maximilians-University (Munich, Germany) in spring 2022. Materials from the holdings of the university's extensive collection, along with those of the German National Library (Leipzig), the State Libraries in

Bavaria and Berlin, the City Archives in Nuremberg, the Institute for War, Holocaust, and Genocide Studies (Netherlands), the Wiener Holocaust Library (United Kingdom), and Yad Vashem (Israel) contribute to this revised edition, and I appreciate the invaluable work of librarians and archivists such as Margaret Fast, Gerhard Jochem, Leibl Rosenberg, and Howard Falksohn in making an array of sources available to me. Mentors and friends in Germany and the United States—in particular John K. Roth, whose writings and genuine kindness I greatly admire—contributed time, advice, and encouragement during my year-long sabbatical and beyond. My mother-in-law, Freya Partsch, lent a helping hand by transcribing select diary entries and letters from their original *Sütterlin* into Latin script. Finally, to my parents, Insa and Karl-Heinz, my brother and sister-in-law, Patrick and Anika, my niece and nephew, Annalena and Emilian, and my husband, Cornelius Partsch: Your love sustains me. It is to you that I dedicate this book.

The Life and Work of Else Dormitzer

Portrait of Else Dormitzer, 1877–1958.

View of Nuremberg's city center with its synagogue before 1938.

Introduction

Nuremberg. The name of this medieval German city conjures up images of the Nazi past like few others—from the massive, frenzied crowds at the National Socialist Party rallies of the 1930s to the Allied trials of Hitler's henchmen at the International Military Tribunal in 1945/46. A set of laws better known today as the Nuremberg Race Laws of 1935 codified the exclusion of German Jews from society by depriving them of their legal rights as citizens. Based on bogus racial theories that legally inscribed racial difference and inferiority to a mere 0.77% of the total German population (1933), they were but one stepping stone in the radicalization of government-issued decrees, paving the way for further unchecked persecution and violence.[1]

As early as 1923, Julius Streicher, then an elementary schoolteacher in Nuremberg keen on gaining political power in the internal struggles of a not yet unified right-wing movement in Bavaria, started publishing his weekly tabloid *Der Stürmer*, brazenly broadcasting his antisemitic tirades. By the time the Nuremberg Race Laws went into effect, Streicher was in control of one of Germany's most successful news outlets. Read widely across the Reich, the National Socialists strategically placed large public display cases for the papers' articles and caricatures at highly frequented spaces in towns and cities, attracting curious passersby who readily consumed the sensationalist and vulgar antisemitic propaganda he and his staff circulated. The city where Streicher's political career took off in the 1920s is also where it came to an end. In 1946, the International Military Tribunal at Nuremberg found him guilty of crimes against humanity, sentencing the former *Frankenführer*, leader of Franconia, to death by hanging.

With good reason, the Nazi past still casts its long shadow over the city's history, its architectural remnants and education sites attracting thousands of visitors each year. There is still much to learn about antisemitism, right-wing politics, and everyday life under a fascist regime steering the

---

1   Bundeszentrale für politische Bildung, "Vertreibung und Deportation der Juden aus dem Deutschen Reich," accessed December 2, 2022, https://www.bpb.de/fsd/centropa/ judenindeutschland1933_1939.php.

country towards war and, eventually, systematic mass murder. But there is also another story to be told alongside that of the perpetrators: one of German-Jewish life, community, and resilience. When visitors encounter these traces in Nuremberg and other towns across Franconia, they are often surprised to learn of the region's sizeable pre-war Jewish communities and their century-old history with "diverse and significant cultural traditions, eminent scholars, specific religious rites, Franconian-Jewish dialects, particular culinary traditions, remarkably many synagogues, and more than one hundred Jewish cemeteries."[2] To reduce the significant thousand-year history to the period between 1933 and 1945 would thus mean obscuring Jewish life past and present in all its forms and complexities; at worst, it would displace or even erase this memory altogether.

This book places aspects of the multifaceted German-Jewish experience before, during, and after the Shoah front and center by introducing the work and life of a woman from Nuremberg: Else Dormitzer (1877–1958). A children's book author, journalist, and political activist, Dormitzer worked tirelessly to advance women's rights in the local Jewish community and on the national level for various organizations, breaking gender barriers as a staunch advocate for women's participation in the fight against antisemitism. Her story is a complex account of female participation in the cultural, religious, social, and political processes of the late nineteenth and early twentieth century, one marked by traditions and innovations, continuities and ruptures, consistencies and contradictions. While forever changed by the events of 1933–1945, her life and work cannot be limited to them—even though it is her writing from and about that period that first introduced me to her.

The Book behind This Book

A little more than three weeks after American Forces blew up the bombastic swastika at the Nazi Party rally grounds during their victory parade on April 22, 1945, Else Dormitzer passed through the ruins of the city she once called home. Part of a convoy of Dutch Holocaust survivors from the Theresienstadt ghetto, the sixty-seven-year-old—hoping to be reunited with family in the Netherlands and the United Kingdom—could hardly believe

---

2 My translation. Michael Brenner and Daniela F. Eisenstein, "Einführung," in *Die Juden in Franken*, ed. Michael Brenner and Daniela F. Eisenstein (Munich: Oldenbourg, 2012), 1.

her eyes. The city lay in ruins. Its old town center, with its beautiful structures and small alleys, was destroyed, the splendor of the Imperial Castle on the hill no longer recognizable. "We drove through the Franconian Switzerland," she later recalled in London, "and I knew that we would soon reach Nuremberg, but I did not recognize the pile of rubble that was once a city. I was not able to speak as we passed through."[3]

Among the few personal belongings in her possession after two years of internment in Theresienstadt were her German-language ghetto diary and poems. In the fall of 1945, she published a selection of these as *Theresienstädter Bilder* (Pictures from Theresienstadt) in a small Dutch press, the collection garnering praise in newspapers such as the New York-based *Aufbau* and bulletins like the one below from the Wiener Holocaust Library in London.[4]

> Fresh and unusual evidence of the indomitable strength of the human spirit is given in several recently published collections of verse. It is the poetry of the fighting, the suffering, and persecuted—poetry under oppression, in ghettos and concentration camps, poetry even in the face of the gas chamber. We feel that these verses are as "documentary" as anything the Library possesses.[5]

A copy of Dormitzer's book first fell into my hands when I researched German-language poetry written in Theresienstadt between 1941 and 1945.[6] As in other ghettos and camps throughout Nazi-occupied Europe, prisoners

---

3   Else Dormitzer, "Experiences in Nuremberg, Holland, Theresienstadt, and during the Transport back to Holland," Wiener Holocaust Library, P.III.h. (Theresienstadt), no. 41. There are three eyewitness accounts in the holdings of the Wiener Holocaust Library; this one is cited throughout this book as "Experiences." See the appendix for the original document in German and its English translation by Cornelius Partsch.

4   Else Dormitzer, *Theresienstädter Bilder* (Hilversum: De Boekenvriend, 1945).

5   Materials from the family's extensive personal archive form the basis of the book; among them are Else Dormitzer's notebooks, in which this short article is included as a paper clipping, *The Wiener Library Bulletin*, September 1947.

6   See the bibliography for my publications on the subject. While working on my dissertation, I came across Dormitzer's poetry collection and testimonial accounts in the holdings of Yad Vashem (Israel) that Ruth Schwertfeger analyzes along with other texts in her study *Women of Theresienstadt. Voices from a Concentration Camp* (New York: St. Martin's Press, 1989). Schwertfeger translated nine poems from *Theresienstädter Bilder* (Pictures from Theresienstadt) and included them in her book; there are ten altogether. She also translated select passages from the testimonial accounts.

often turned to writing poetry as a means of giving voice to their varied traumatic experiences in languages such as Dutch, French, Polish, and Yiddish. My work as a literary scholar focuses on German-language poetry from the Holocaust and investigates the marginalization of camp poetry within German academic discourses on Holocaust literature after 1945. While primarily viewed as a language of perpetration, it was also, of course, the mother tongue of Jewish communities in the German-speaking world, most prominently in Austria and Germany.

In my studies, I draw on the rich transnational and transdisciplinary body of Anglo-American scholarship on literature and testimony and offer a framework in which to read these texts as instances of early victim testimony, highlighting the specific context and circumstances of poetic production. A Germanist by trade, my work has aimed at intervening primarily in German Studies, which continues to relegate poetry from the Holocaust to the sidelines of scholarly inquiry by deeming it aesthetically inferior in comparison to texts written after 1945. This literary devaluation which evolved in the early 1950s in light of Theodor W. Adorno's often (mis)quoted dictum, "to write poetry after Auschwitz is barbaric," still holds a powerful grip today and has led—with few exceptions—to the exclusion of studies on camp poetry within the broader context of German-language literature of and about the Shoah.[7] It can be interpreted, I argue, as a conscious attempt by West German academia shortly after the end of World War II to depoliticize literature in an effort to avoid its own confrontation with an uncomfortable past and its entanglements with a murderous regime between 1933 and 1945. Ultimately, this form of aesthetic cleansing allowed a second silencing of victims' voices. As a result, poetry written "under oppression, in ghettos and concentration camps, poetry even in the face of the gas chamber" remains at the periphery of scholarly inquiry and literary culture, where it serves to sustain the project of installing a German myth of having come to terms with its past.

---

7   Theodor W. Adorno, "Kulturkritik und Gesellschaft," in idem *Gesammelte Schriften*, volume 10, part 1, ed. Rolf Tiedemann (Frankfurt am Main: Suhrkamp, 1996), 16. One such recent exception, for example, is an edited volume on literature from the camps that appeared in 2021. Saskia Fischer, Mareike Gronich, and Joanna Bednarska-Kociolek, eds., *Lagerliteratur. Schreibweisen, Zeugnisse, Didaktik* (Berlin: Peter Lang, 2021). At the Justus-Liebig-University Giessen, the *Arbeitsstelle Holocaustliteratur* (Institute on Holocaust Literature) is dedicated to collecting and disseminating Holocaust and concentration camp literature, fostering interdisciplinary research and teaching. Also see their website, accessed August 22, 2023: https://www.holocaustliteratur.de/english/.

When a former colleague of mine at Dickinson College in Pennsylvania, Michael Heiman, invited me to present my research at a reunion of the Nuremberg-Fürth Survivors Group in 2008, I decided to share my work by highlighting Else Dormitzer and her collection of poetry from Theresienstadt. Founded in the United States in 1977 by Frank Harris, the Nuremberg-Fürth Survivors Group is a global network of Franconian Holocaust survivors and their descendants, gathering every few years for reunions with friends and families. Until his passing in 2017, Frank Harris—born Franz Siegmund Hess in Fürth in 1922— sent out an annual newsletter reaching more than 1,200 recipients on all five continents, often accompanied by his signature sticky notes with personalized messages.[8] Up until the "Five Generations-One Community" reunion in New York State, I had not been successful in gathering much biographical information on Dormitzer, but two women familiar with her life happened to be in the audience the afternoon I gave my talk, and started filling in the gaps. Before we left Ellenville, Claudia Strauss and her mother Lore (née Seidenberger) provided me with a family tree that proved of great value for my work.[9] I occasionally corresponded with Claudia and Frank after the gathering, receiving the group's newsletter each fall, but I directed my attention to other projects at the time. In 2012, however, as I considered revisiting Dormitzer's poetry collection, I contacted Frank to ask if he could help me locate any further living relatives by placing a call in his newsletter. And so he did.

Not long after publishing the request, I received a message from Paris from a man called Gérard Langlois, who, as I learned, was the son of a former business partner of Else Dormitzer's son-in-law Ernst Rosenfelder and a very close family friend.[10] He had read the entry. A telephone conversation followed in which I further explained the nature of my studies before he connected me with Else Dormitzer's great-grandson, Thomas Runkel (Germany), and her two grandsons, Henk Haas (Netherlands) and George Rogers (United Kingdom). We corresponded, first over e-mail for several months, and then

8 Gerhard Jochem, "Biography of Frank A. Harris, Fürth," accessed March 17, 2022, http://www.rijo.homepage.t-online.de/pdf/en_fu_ju_Harris_Frank.pdf.

9 For information on Lore Strauss see the following webpage: "Lore Strauss," accessed November 15, 2022, https://hhrecny.org/holocaust-survivor-speakers/lore-strauss/.

10 Gérard Langlois, "Histoire de la famille Löwensohn," accessed April 20, 2022, http://www.rijo.homepage.t-online.de/pdf/FR_FU_JU_loewensohn.pdf.

in the winter of 2013, I accepted the invitation to meet with family members in their homes and traveled to Germany and the Netherlands.

It soon became evident that *Theresienstädter Bilder* was but one of Dormitzer's many publications. Day after day, boxes and folders filled with primary materials appeared as the family opened their extensive, yet not complete, personal archive to me, starting to place the original book of poetry into context: children's books, newspaper clippings and articles, essays, personal notebooks and loose papers, calendars, letters, postcards from Theresienstadt, Red Cross telegrams from the Netherlands and the United Kingdom, records from the Jewish Council in Amsterdam, photographs, the family's guest books dating back to 1898, a diary from Theresienstadt, and three post-war accounts; an astonishing array of invaluable documents in German, Dutch, and English. In the following months and years, the family permitted me to work closely with materials in their possession. After further research in the German National Library in Leipzig, the State Library in Berlin, the City Archives in Nuremberg, the Institute for War, Holocaust, and Genocide Studies in Amsterdam (NIOD), and with assistance from the Wiener Holocaust Library in London and Yad Vashem in Jerusalem, I was able to piece Else Dormitzer's extraordinary life together and share her story with her family for the first time. I published the results, including Dormitzer's Theresienstadt poems and her three testimonial accounts, as *weiter schreiben. Leben und Lyrik der Else Dormitzer* in 2015 with Hentrich & Hentrich in Berlin (now Leipzig), a press specializing in Jewish culture and history.[11] The project, which had started with the original book of poetry from 1945, had come full circle.

Who was Else Dormitzer?

At a time when "society expected a smattering of intelligence and polish—but no more—from its women," Else Dormitzer was a successful writer, journalist, and activist.[12] Born and raised in Nuremberg, she authored at least twenty-nine children's books until the early 1930s under the pseudonym Else Dorn. Once women were permitted to become members in political

---

11 Sandra Alfers, *weiter schreiben. Leben und Lyrik der Else Dormitzer* (Berlin: Hentrich & Hentrich, 2015).

12 Marion A. Kaplan, *The Making of the Jewish Middle Class: Women, Family, and Identity in Imperial Germany* (New York: Oxford University Press, 1991), 9.

organizations, clubs, and associations in 1908, she joined the Association for Liberal Judaism in Germany and the Central Union of German Citizens of Jewish Faith, becoming an ardent advocate for women's participation in the fight against antisemitism. She regularly published essays and articles in various magazines and newspapers, including *Liberal Judaism* and the *Jewish-Liberal Newspaper*, and gave public talks—many geared towards a female audience—on combatting antisemitism nationwide. Elected to the national board of the Central Union in 1919, she was one of only three women serving in this capacity in the early 1920s—and the only one without a university degree. Her volunteer work, for which she received no compensation, did not stop there. At home, Dormitzer was actively engaged in the local Jewish community, serving on committees, and initiating, for example, the popular *Nuremberg Israelite Community Paper* (1921–1938) with support from the congregation's leadership. Breaking the glass ceiling once again, she held an elected position on the Jewish community board since 1922, according to Nuremberg historian Leibl Rosenberg, "the first woman in German Judaism" in such a position in all of Weimar Germany.[13]

In the 1920s, Nuremberg became central to Nazi propaganda, and the local Jewish community increasingly became the target of violent antisemitism. The National Socialists held their first party rally in 1927 and expanded the social and political mass gatherings in subsequent years. In the summer of 1938, months before their nationwide anti-Jewish terror attack also known as *Kristallnacht* or *Reichspogromnacht*, the Nuremberg city administration ordered the demolition of the main synagogue in the center of town—in the eyes of Mayor Willy Liebel, "the city's greatest architectural sin"—in a celebrated public act.[14] When a mob of about fifteen men destroyed much

---

13 Leibl Rosenberg, *Spuren und Fragmente. Jüdische Schicksale in Nürnberg* (Nuremberg: Israelitische Kultusgemeinde und die Stadt Nürnberg, 2000), 127.

14 My translation. Bernhard Kolb, *Die Juden in Nürnberg 1839–1945*, ed. Gerhard Jochem, accessed February 6, 2022, http://www.rijo.homepage.t-online.de/pdf/DE_NU_JU_kolb_text.pdf. In the German language, the violent attacks of November 9 and 10, 1938, are generally referred to as *Reichspogromnacht* and not *Kristallnacht* since the terms *Kristallnacht* or *Reichskristallnacht* are viewed as euphemisms. "The word pogrom comes from Russian ('погром'). It emerged in the 1880s during the czarist Russian Empire to designate massacres of Jews. Literally, pogrom means 'devastation' or 'riot.' In Germany, the term pogrom has become a widespread designation for the events of 9–10 November 1938. However, because 'pogrom' signifies an act of violence initiated by the common people, its use is in danger of hiding the state's central role in planning and directing the violent actions of 9–10 November 1938. The term *Kristallnacht*

of the Dormitzers' property during the night of November 9, 1938, severely injuring Else's husband, Dr. Jur. Sigmund Dormitzer (1869–1943), their daughters, Dr. Jur. Hildegard Haas (1907–1988) and Elisabeth Rosenfelder (1899–1977) finally convinced the parents to leave Germany for good, as they had done earlier. Securing one of the 8,000 special immigration permits issued by the Dutch government after the November pogrom, Hildegard and her husband Richard (1908–1983) welcomed them into their home in Hilversum in the spring of 1939, only a few months before the outbreak of World War II in Europe.

After the German occupation of the Netherlands in May 1940, the family lived in constant upheaval and escalating danger, moving from one place to another as they tried evading deportation. On April 21, 1943, the German authorities put Else and Sigmund Dormitzer on the first transport from Amsterdam to Theresienstadt, Transport XXIV/1. As her diary and an original postcard from Theresienstadt reveal, Sigmund died in Theresienstadt in December of the same year. In the ghetto, she became actively involved in the Office for Leisure-Time Activities and delivered public presentations on a broad range of subjects. According to her notes, she gave 275 talks,

---

(or *Reichskristallnacht*), meaning Night of Crystal (i.e., broken glass), as the non-Jewish majority called the acts of terror, is generally avoided in German today because it is a euphemism. It only references the physical damage, specifically broken windows and crystal chandeliers. The word 'night' (the -*nacht* in *Kristallnacht*) is also misleading because the violent acts continued by the light of day. Internationally, particularly in English, *Kristallnacht* is an established term. From a Jewish perspective and in the memories of eyewitnesses to these events, this word is often still used to describe the events of 9 and 10 November 1938. Meanwhile, propaganda terms such as *Judenaktion* (Jewish Action) clearly belong to the language of the perpetrators." "9 November 1938/ Kristallnacht," Jewish Museum Berlin, accessed August 22, 2023, https://www.jmberlin.de/en/topic-9-november-1938. Else Dormitzer uses *Kristallnacht* to describe the terror she experienced, which is in line with early responses; it is also the title of one of her testimonial accounts included in this book. More recently, Ulrich Baumann and François Guesnet have argued that the term *Pogromnacht* is also misleading since it does not sufficiently reflect the "coordinated and systematic attack of a depraved regime on a defenseless minority." They point out that the events were "planned, organized, centrally triggered and executed, to the most devastating of effects," and therefore suggest terms such as "November terror," "anti-Jewish terror," or "state terror" as more precise linguistic alternatives when describing or referring to the events. Ulrich Baumann and François Guesnet, "Kristallnacht-Pogrom-State Terror: A Terminological Reflection," in *New Perspectives on Kristallnacht: After 80 Years, the Nazi Pogrom in Global Comparison*, ed. Steven J. Ross, Wolf Gruner, and Lisa Ansell (West Lafayette: Purdue University Press, 2019), 15.

"many of them for the elderly and sick. I was among the few who did not shy away from speaking in all sections of the tuberculosis ward, and the patients appreciated this greatly."[15] Else also wrote poetry and shared it with fellow prisoners. It seems as if she chronicled much of her life during the war on a day-to-day basis, but a diary from 1943, a few pages from the summer of 1945, and her poetry written in Theresienstadt are all that remain with her immediate family.

Else Dormitzer returned to the Netherlands in the summer of 1945 and, from then on, she spent half of the year in the Netherlands with the Haas family, who had also survived, and the other half in the United Kingdom with the Rosenfelders. She became a British citizen in 1951. In London, she joined the New Liberal Jewish Congregation and started shaping and participating in community life, for example, as an editorial team member of the community newsletter *Our Congregation* or as a contributor of short essays to the *Synagogue Review* and *AJR Review*. She also led a conversation group for survivors. In 1952, Else returned for a visit to her former hometown, followed thereafter by short annual trips to Franconia until she died in London in 1958.

A Note on Content, Organization, and Language

This book traces Else Dormitzer's life and work in five chapters; it situates the pre-war, war, and post-war years in local and national contexts and makes available her original poetry collection from Theresienstadt along with three testimonial reports in German and English for the first time. A revised edition of the German original *weiter schreiben. Leben und Lyrik der Else Dormitzer*, the biographical account has been rewritten with an English-language readership in mind, incorporating new findings and benefiting from content reorganization. Words in languages other than English are italicized for better recognition—except for the names Theresienstadt/Terezín—and English translations of quotes from primary and secondary sources provided. All chapters are designed around their geographic locales, firmly anchoring Dormitzer's biography in socio-historical and sociocultural frameworks. Except for the first chapter, which recounts her return to the Netherlands and reintegration into post-war society, I follow a chronological sequence, taking

---

15 Dormitzer, "Experiences."

the reader from Germany to the Netherlands (Hilversum/Amsterdam), the Czech Republic (Theresienstadt), and the United Kingdom (London). A selection of family pictures, images of documents, and official photographs supplements individual sections.

Spanning just a few months, the first chapter (Hilversum and London, 1945–1946) has the two-fold purpose of introducing family members while highlighting the importance of writing from the beginning of Dormitzer's story. It sets the stage for a detailed account of the development of both her private and public life in chapter two (Nuremberg, 1877–1939), which covers more than fifty years and provides a window into the complexities of a German-Jewish woman's life in Imperial Germany, the Weimar Republic, and the Third Reich. Topics cover motherhood and family life, community work and activism, and finding one's way as a minority in a majority society that became increasingly hostile as the years progressed, resulting in the Dormitzers' flight to the Netherlands in March 1939. Until their deportation to Theresienstadt in April 1943, Sigmund and Else Dormitzer created a new home in the Netherlands, trying to navigate the difficulties of living in a foreign environment and learning a new language as elderly refugees. Chapter three (Hilversum and Amsterdam, 1939–1943) illustrates this adjustment and shows the family's efforts in creating and maintaining a sense of normalcy under continuously deteriorating circumstances beyond their control. Covering the time from April 1943 to June 1945, the fourth chapter (Theresienstadt, 1943–1945) centers on the couples' internment and places particular emphasis on the function and organization of cultural activities in the ghetto, highlighting the role of poetry in Theresienstadt in particular and during the Holocaust in general. I also provide a close reading of Dormitzer's texts not only to broaden and deepen our understanding of the multifaceted experience of everyday life in the ghetto and its literary representation but also to close a gap in research since poetry continues to be overlooked in conversations on the cultural life of the ghetto. Finally, the last chapter (London, 1946–1958) summarizes what is known of the post-war years, showing her unceasing intellectual engagement and creative spirit in her ongoing writing. The appendix contains the poetry collection *Pictures from Theresienstadt* and the three testimonial accounts "Else Dormitzer: Experiences in Nuremberg, Holland, Theresienstadt, and during the Transport back to Holland," "Life in Theresienstadt," and "The Night of Broken Glass" in both German and English, with translations provided by Cornelius Partsch. A bibliography, including a list of Dormitzer's primary works, closes the book.

Traces of Memory is based primarily on the wealth of multilingual materials from the family archive and amended for context by socio-historical and sociocultural sources. It employs the terms "ghetto" and "camp" as well as the names "Theresienstadt" and "Terezín" interchangeably without intending to discard or modulate their particularities. Based on the often overlapping functions ascribed to the Theresienstadt ghetto between 1941–1945, historians have long debated its categorization as a ghetto, camp, or transit camp with the Czech original Terezín often used in reference to the town's name before the German repurposing of Theresienstadt between 1941 and 1945 as "a link in the chain that inevitably led to the gas chambers."[16] My previous work has itself been informed by these conversations and included different classifications. Else Dormitzer describes Theresienstadt both as a ghetto and as a concentration camp, and, while this characterization may be imprecise for historians, the underlying perception is nevertheless critical in revealing the implicit power dynamics by the dual naming conventions while simultaneously pointing to the complexities inherent to Theresienstadt/Terezín as a transnational space for European Jews during the Nazi occupation of Bohemia and Moravia. For the same reason, but in a departure from the German original, I use the terms Holocaust and Shoah interchangeably in the English version, being cognizant and mindful of the denotation of national contexts, particularities, and sensibilities implied by these terms. Finally, in close mirroring of the German-language original much of this book is written in the present tense. While the simple past is a more common choice in English-language books, my keeping with the present tense intends to create a vivid and descriptive retelling of Else Dormitzer's life, unfolding before the readers' eyes as they follow along on the pages. Sixty-six years after her death, I hope this book successfully conveys the significance of her contributions to German-Jewish history and memory.

---

16 Sybil Milton, "Art in the Context of Theresienstadt," in *Art, Music, Education as Strategies for Survival: Theresienstadt*, ed. Anne Dutlinger (New York: Herodias, 2000), 18.

Hilversum, Netherlands, in the summer of 1945, from left to right: Dr. Hildegard Haas, Richard Haas with son Henk, Else Dormitzer. Photograph included in a letter from Else Dormitzer to Fred Lessing.

CHAPTER ONE

Hilversum and London, 1945–1946

> "It seems like a miracle to me that we were able
> to escape the witches' cauldron; I would have <u>never</u>
> thought it possible."

On October 2, 1945, five months after liberation from the Theresienstadt ghetto, Else Dormitzer includes these lines in a letter to her great-nephew, Fred Lessing, in New York City.[1] She has returned to the Netherlands, the country to which she fled with her husband in 1939, to be reunited with her youngest daughter Dr. Jur. Hildegard Haas (1907–1988), and her family. As best as she can, the sixty-seven-year-old is trying to adjust to the realities of post-war life. In the family's house in Hilversum, only a short distance from Amsterdam, she spends hours on end writing letter after letter in the hopes of reconnecting with family and friends. A few short months after the end of the war, she is eager to learn about the fate of loved ones: her extended family, her large circle of friends, old and new acquaintances.

While she and her nephew did indeed escape the "witches' cauldron," others did not, including her husband of more than fifty years, Dr. Jur. Sigmund Dormitzer (1869–1943), and Fred's parents. Not only does the American nephew reply with thoughtful letters to his aunt's detailed reports, but he also regularly sends care packages to her and other surviving family members, containing an assortment of goods. From food items such as sugar, canned sausages, lard, and dried figs, to everyday objects like clothes, soles,

---

1   Unless otherwise noted, quotes in the main text of this chapter are from documents in the personal archive of surviving family members. All translations, including secondary materials unavailable in English, are mine.

boots, and, yes, bicycle tires and tubes. In sum, Fred sends anything he can get his hands on to make life for his relatives in post-war Europe more bearable and comfortable. His stamps from the US Postal Service do double duty: they get his letters across the Atlantic, and the unused American stamp series Fred includes in his mailings serve his aunt as a way "to complement her small allowance." Now financially reliant on her two children, Else sells them for cash at the local stamp exchange and contributes the funds to offset the costs of everyday life. It is by no means easy for her to get used to this dependency since she and her husband were the ones prior to World War II with financial means and decision-making power. At least, that is, until the German government disowns them in 1938, stealing their property and expropriating their assets.

Fred Lessing also takes care of the spiritual nourishment of his relatives, sending copies of *Life Magazine* and a subscription to the *Aufbau*, the famous German-language newspaper published in New York for German-speaking Jews around the world. Else reads both with immense interest. The *Aufbau* regularly publishes lists with names of Holocaust survivors and prints personal ads by those seeking missing family members, relatives, and friends. Wherever possible, she tries to help, contacting those looking for information in writing. In Theresienstadt, she kept an extensive notebook containing information about fellow prisoners during her two years of internment. Over 800 people are included in this personal registry. "I have received countless inquiries from around the world for information on relatives and friends from Theresienstadt," she writes in the spring of 1946 to her nephew, "and my correspondence has indeed grown so much that I cannot answer them all." At this time, she is already in London with her eldest daughter Elisabeth Rosenfelder (1899–1977), and her family. In the evenings, granddaughter Dora (1922–2019) is lending a helping hand as a personal assistant, patiently typing her grandmother's dictations to help her manage the extensive correspondence.

A few months prior, Else mailed one of the first existing post-war photos of herself and the Hilversum family to Fred, a "snapshot that shows you that these four emaciated apparitions will tremendously enjoy your nutritious and carefully selected food and will do so with deep gratitude." While her four-year-old grandson Henk (1941) is smiling mischievously into the camera, the years of persecution and war are written in the faces of the adults. Pictured alongside Henk are Else, Hildegard, and son-in-law Richard Haas (1908–1983). "I was deeply shocked when I first saw her,"

Hildegard writes to her sister in London after seeing her mother for the first time in July 1945,

> so bad that I would not have known her if I had met her in some other place. I saw that she is not changed mentally, only very nervous, of course, but the first impression was awful, like one of the photos from the concentration camps of the hunger ghosts.[2]

With support from her family, who do all they can to make life as pleasant and easy for her as possible, Else soon regains her physical strength and incredible mental agility. She continues to do what has always sustained her: writing, and the family gives her space to do so. In a matter of months, she succeeds in connecting to her varied pre-war publication record by finding a publishing house for her German-language poems from the Theresienstadt ghetto. The small Dutch press De Boekenvriend takes on her collection, and the book appears as *Theresienstädter Bilder* in the fall of 1945. Costs: 2½ Dutch guilders per volume; 500 books in total. Around the same time, she also starts speaking publicly about her experience during the Holocaust, giving lectures about "Life in Theresienstadt," first in Hilversum and later in London. Family members are trying to secure the necessary visa documents for travel to England, along with the required exit permit from the Dutch authorities, so that Else can be reunited with Elisabeth and family. Finally, the papers come through, and preparations for the upcoming departure begin to consume her everyday activities. Taking up considerable space in her luggage are numerous writing materials, including her personal registry from Theresienstadt and her ghetto diary. After years of separation, she joyfully embraces Elisabeth, Dora, and son-in-law Ernst Rosenfelder (1894–1976) in their house on Mount Pleasant Road in London in December 1945. Grandson Albert (1925), who joined the 11th Armored Divison of the British Army in 1943 and is stationed in Northern Germany at the time of his grandmother's arrival, cannot welcome her personally. However, on December 24, 1945, he sends a telegram from his post abroad: "Welcome Home! Hope to see you soon. Merry Christmas to all! Love, Albert."

---

2   Quote from Hildegard Haas's original letter, which is in English.

The Rosenfelder family fled Germany for the United Kingdom in the summer of 1938, and Ernst is about to restart his career in publishing in London after the end of the war in 1945. In 1919, he had taken on and expanded the business of the well-known German children's and picture book publisher G. Löwensohn in Nuremberg. His friends and business partners, Robert and Gustav Löwensohn, are dead—Robert killed on a death march from the Blechhammer forced labor camp (Poland) in the vicinity of today's Mościsko (Poland), and Gustav in Auschwitz (Poland).[3] Neither Ernst nor Elisabeth want to leave England and return to Nuremberg, and it is difficult for the family to comprehend the decision by their newly married daughter Dora and her husband Rolf Runkel (1905–1975) to leave their new home and settle in Düsseldorf, Germany. Somewhat reluctantly and with significant worries, Else sees them off in October 1946. She herself does not visit her once beloved hometown until a few years later. A permanent return to Franconia is off the table, although the family has deep roots in the region.

---

3   Robert Löwensohn was Gérard Langlois's father. Blechhammer labor camp was a subcamp of Auschwitz, established on April 1, 1944. "The Germans began evacuating the prisoners on January 21, 1945, in connection with the Russian winter offensive. Approximately 4,000 prisoners were driven on foot to Gross-Rosen, which was reached ten days later. Weak prisoners who did not keep up in the march were shot along the way. Prisoners estimate that approximately 800 people were killed on the way. Mass graves of several dozen bodies each were found along the evacuation route after liberation." Franciszek Piper, "Blechhammer," trans. Gerard Majka, in *The United States Holocaust Memorial Museum Encyclopedia of Ghettos and Camps: Early Camps, Youth Camps, Concentration Camps and Subcamps under the SS-Business Administration Office*, volume 1, part A, ed. Geoffrey P. Megargee (Bloomington: Indiana University Press, 2009), 228.

View of the synagogue with its main entrance from *Spitalplatz* in Nuremberg, today's Hans-Sachs-Square.

Side view of the synagogue in the center of Nuremberg from the Pegnitz river.

CHAPTER TWO

Nuremberg, 1877–1939

Born November 17, 1877, as Else Forchheimer, Else is the older of two daughters. Her parents, Salomon (1848–1904) and Clara (née Ehrlich, 1856–1936), are originally from Bamberg, a small town about thirty-five miles north of Nuremberg in the upper Franconia region of Bavaria.[1] Else's father, Salomon Forchheimer, is a successful merchant in one of Germany's oldest medieval and, in the 1880s, fastest-growing trade cities, counting close to 100,000 inhabitants around the time of Else's birth. He owns a sawmill and trades in wholesale in the region's traditional hop and timber industries.

Representing the emerging German-Jewish middle class, his family participates actively in community life and charity work. The Forchheimers are members of the local congregation, the *Israelitische Kultusgemeinde*, founded in 1862. Centrally located and adjacent to the city's main town square, the community's newly built synagogue on *Spitalplatz* (today's *Hans-Sachs-Platz*) opens its doors to congregants in 1874. Twenty-four years prior, in 1850, the Nuremberg city administration narrowly passed a vote allowing German Jews to take up residency within its town limits, the first time in nearly four hundred years. Mirroring practice in several cities across the German lands, King Maximilian had expelled the city's Jewish residents in 1499 in coordination with the city administration and the church, despite—or rather precisely because of—their contributions to Nuremberg's economic growth and, ultimately, its reputation as a merchant powerhouse.[2] Now, between 1880 and

---

1   Unless otherwise noted, quotes in the main text of this chapter are from documents in the personal archive of surviving family members. Cornelius Partsch translated the three testimonial accounts and poetry collection. All other translations, including secondary materials unavailable in English, are mine.

2   Arnd Müller, *Geschichte der Juden in Nürnberg 1146–1946* (Nuremberg: Selbstverlag der Stadtbibliothek Nürnberg, 1968), 79.

1925, the Jewish community in Nuremberg, whose roots can be traced back to as early as 1146, is growing, however, never reaching more than three percent of the population.[3]

The constitution of the newly established German Reich in 1871 finally unites a conglomerate of thirty states and state-like entities into a nation of one, granting civil rights to all German Jews for the first time. Since its legal implementation lies in the hands of individual states, however, social barriers and century-old restrictions—for example, the choice for German Jews to take up any profession without restriction or regulation—are only slowly and partly being eliminated. Ongoing political debates in regional legislative sessions continuously draw into question the basic need to extend equality to German Jews in the first place, attempting to undo and undermine the newly established national laws.[4] At the same time, right-wing groups, ultra-nationalist organizations, and political parties are stirring up modern-day antisemitism by using familiar anti-Jewish tropes and stereotypes that can be easily instrumentalized during the unstable economic situation of the last third of the nineteenth century. These groups eventually succeed in labeling German Jews as foreign, alien elements, questioning their Germanness and, thus, their loyalty to the German nation.[5] The struggle for unrestricted civil rights for a minority that never makes up more than one percent of the total population remains unsuccessful until the end of World War I in 1918, when the constitution of the Weimar Republic finally grants them in full and without exception.[6]

---

3   For exact numbers see Georg Seiderer, "Entwicklungslinien jüdischer Geschichte in Nürnberg von der Wiederansiedlung bis zur Weimarer Republik," in *Geschichte und Kultur der Juden in Nürnberg*, ed. Andrea M. Kluxen and Julia Krieger (Würzburg: Ergon, 2014), 166. Gerhard Jochem bases his estimation on Kolb's *Die Juden in Nürnberg 1839–1945*. In 1875, Nuremberg has approximately 91,018 inhabitants, and 2,7% of the total population (2,453 inhabitants) is Jewish.

4   In Bavaria, for example, lawmakers intentionally break the new German constitution by introducing a quota in parliament to limit the number of Jewish lawyers. See Reinhard Weber, "Berufliche Ausgrenzungen von jüdischen Rechtsanwälten und Justizbediensteten," in *Entrechtet. Entwürdigt. Beraubt. Die Arisierung in Nürnberg und Fürth*, ed. Matthias Henkel and Eckart Dietzfelbinger (Petersberg: Michael Imhof, 2021), 84.

5   Cornelia Hecht, *Deutsche Juden und Antisemitismus in der Weimarer Republik* (Bonn: Dietz, 2003), 36–37.

6   Arno Herzig, "1815–1933: Emanzipation und Akkulturation," in *Jüdisches Leben in Deutschland*, August 5, 2010, accessed December 19, 2021. https://www.bpb.de/shop/zeitschriften/izpb/7674/1815-1933-emanzipation-und-akkulturation.

Else's mother, Clara Forchheimer, is raising her daughter to be a confident young woman. Else attends the higher girls' school in Heidelberg but is barred from continuing her education at university in Bavaria after graduation; the state only grants this right to women in 1903. While denied to her, it is simply unthinkable for Else that her daughters a generation later would not continue their formal education at university. Growing up, she develops a passion for music and the sciences; Else loves to read and play the piano, and as a young woman, she enthusiastically starts supporting the goals of the growing women's movement. On May 1, 1898, the twenty-year-old marries Sigmund Dormitzer, eight years her senior. Sigmund is an aspiring young lawyer, also having been raised in a bourgeois family. Like the majority of German Jews around the turn of the century, the young couple identifies with Progressive Judaism; they do not see their spiritual home in Orthodox Judaism, nor do they find their ideological home in Zionism. Rather, they are proud of the accomplishments of the German-Jewish Reform movement, which understands itself as part of the young German nation, seeking full equal rights as citizens without loss of their Jewish identity. As Leibl Rosenberg writes in an essay about the Dormitzer family: "Naturally, one was Jewish and *nürnbergerisch*—one was, of course, cosmopolitan, and participated in the city's social life—just like any other citizens."[7]

After a magnificent wedding in 1898, the newlyweds move close to old town Nuremberg, to *Blumenstraße*, located just outside the medieval ring of the city and in proximity to the city center and central train station. Until the end of the 1920s, they live on the first floor of *Blumenstraße* 1; in 1930, at the latest, they move a few houses down to *Blumenstraße* 9. Belonging to the Forchheimer family, the property borders the *Goldbach*, a tributary of the Pegnitz River, in the back. The couple moves into the eight-room apartment on the ground floor of the two-story home. Else's younger sister, Marie Ottenstein (1880–1947), and husband Julius (1874–1943) live upstairs with their only son Hans (1902–1986). From there, it is only a few minutes to Sigmund's law office in *Karolinenstraße* 40, a firm that he co-owns with his partner Dr. Jur. Bernhard Eismann.

Sigmund Dormitzer soon builds an excellent professional reputation and holds serval distinguished local positions. From 1916 until 1926, he

---

7   Leibl Rosenberg, *Spuren und Fragmente. Jüdische Schicksale in Nürnberg* (Nuremberg: Israelitische Kultusgemeinde und die Stadt Nürnberg, 2000), 127.

serves as the first chairman of the Nuremberg Lawyers' Association, and from 1926 until March 1933, he is the deputy chairman of the Bar Association at the Higher Regional Court Nuremberg. In 1928, the state of Bavaria honors his accomplishments and contributions to the profession by promoting him from *Justizrat*, councilor of justice (1918), to *Geheimer Justizrat*, privy councilor. His active membership in numerous organizations, for instance, the Aid Organization of German Jews and the local Rotary Club, further illustrates his social, political, and societal engagement. Like other family members, he is actively involved in charity work, supporting various organizations with private funds and his free time; for example, he volunteers as a legal adviser to the Economic Association of Nuremberg Artists. Sigmund's brother Louis (1863–1943), co-owner of a wholesale brush business on *Marienplatz*, lives with his wife Sophie (née Kupfer, 1871–1942) and their children Max and Lilli in nearby *Marienstraße*.

While her husband practices law and fulfills his public and societal obligations outside the home, Else takes on the expected traditional role of mother, housewife, and guardian of the private sphere. The wellbeing of the young family is her responsibility, and she self-confidently sees herself as an equal partner to her husband. As an agent of bourgeois and Jewish-liberal values, it is up to her to raise the daughters, born eight years apart, as educated, independent young women. According to historian Marion Kaplan, Jewish women participate decisively in a multi-layered acculturation process around the turn of the century but face double discrimination.

> The Sabbath and German classics, synagogue and piano lessons, carefully crafted furnishings and German patriotism, Jewish friends and family—these were the separate threads that composed the fabric of middle-class Jewish women's lives in Imperial Germany. Jewish women wove intricate and complicated patterns in designing their environments, choosing from modern bourgeois practice and traditional familial and communal customs. Paradoxically for historians, but perfectly consistently and reasonably for themselves, they were agents of acculturation and tradition, of integration and apartness [...] In sum, a double dilemma confronted Jewish women: they could reach for new goals opened by Jewish emancipation and integration into bourgeois society, and they could strive beyond boundaries that once limited women. Yet they

still suffered from double discrimination based on gender and religion. [...] As women, they never received full legal equality and suffered from economic, political, and social discrimination; as Jews they saw the fruits of emancipation dwindle dramatically with the recurrences of anti-Semitism.[8]

Else takes care of the children, the household, and its daily chores with help from two maids, Retha and Marie. They aid in the cleaning of the apartment and its furniture, help with laundry, buy food from the market and specialty stores, and prepare meals. She also regularly plans and prepares eloquent multi-course dinners for business colleagues, friends, and acquaintances from their social, political, and religious circles, fulfilling her role as the perfect hostess and displaying her organizational talent and hard work. She enjoys participating in the lively conversations around the dinner table, exchanging stories about everyday life in Nuremberg, local politics, the city's cultural events, and the work of local charities.

To this day, three original guest books, dating back to the year of Else and Sigmund's wedding (November 1898), are a testament to the family's extensive participation in public life. In these books, visitors to the home on *Blumenstraße* express their gratitude and appreciation for the wonderful entertainment, the hosts' attention to detail, and the family's generosity. Often, they do so by including drawings or poems. Family members are also among the guests at the various dinner, garden, or tea parties, and it is these family connections that Else values and tends to with great care, for example, by engaging in regular letter correspondence and personal visits whenever possible. Early on, she thus succeeds in building a far-reaching network with people from all walks of life, spanning countries and continents, a network that exists until her death in 1958.

Early Writing, 1900–1914

Despite the demanding tasks of everyday life, Else carves out time for her biggest passion: writing. A versatile and talented writer, she takes an interest in a range of topics and, around the turn of the century, starts placing journalistic pieces of varied length on women's topics, such as children's education

---

8   Kaplan, *The Making of the Jewish Middle Class*, 18–19.

or household management, in local and regional newspapers and magazines, for example, in the *Franconian Courier, General Newspaper Frankfurt*, and the *Magazine for Childcare.*[9] Using her pseudonym Else Dorn she also publishes travel reports and theater reviews, for instance, the "Theater Letter from Nuremberg" in the *Coburg Daily Newspaper* dating back to May 12, 1908.[10]

Among her interests during these early years of writing is a highly unusual subject that raises more than just a few eyebrows from family members and friends. She is actively helping promote the newly created crematoria associations in Germany to garner broad public acceptance for cremation by authoring advocacy pieces in the form of pamphlets and informational brochures. Representing a severe infraction of Jewish religious law, Else Dormitzer takes on a controversial point of view in support of this modern technological burial method which many of her contemporaries find inappropriate for the young woman to pursue. She also contributes articles and essays on the topic to magazines and books, for example, to *Flamma*, a national magazine for the advancement of fire burials, and the chapter "Judaism and Cremation" for the publication *Religion and Cremation* by the Nuremberg Union for Fire Burials.[11] In the latter, she sets out to prove that cremation does not violate Jewish religious law and is, in fact, permissible, concluding: "It needs to be stated explicitly that every Israelite, liberal or conservative, can be cremated without violating the laws or the spirit of religion."[12] In 1916, the local organization recognizes her years of commitment on their behalf by naming her an honorary member. The same year, Dormitzer also edits their twenty-fifth-anniversary publication.

Her fervent contributions in written and spoken word are often subject to sharp criticism and even ridicule, but this does not stop her determination. On the contrary, it appears as if these attacks motivate her even more to continue her efforts boldly. She also does not shy away from the subject during social gatherings at her home. As a guest jokingly writes on September 12, 1910, in one of the family's guest books: "Oh, behold, the guests in this

---

9   *Fränkischer Kurier, Frankfurter Generalanzeiger*, and the *Zeitschrift für Kinderpflege*.
10   *Coburger Tageblatt*.
11   *Flamma: Zeitschrift zur Förderung der Feuerbestattung*; Else Dormitzer, "Judentum und Feuerbestattung," in *Religion und Feuerbestattung*, ed. Nürnberger Feuerbestattungsverein (Nuremberg: Wilh. Tümmels Buchdruckerei, ca. 1912), 12–15.
12   Ibid., 15.

Cover of one of
Else Dormitzer's children's books.

home! Else will surely roast them in the crematorium if they are not born as poets."

Her love for literature and poetry referenced in the guest book entry shines through in the translation and creative writing projects she concurrently develops in the early years of the twentieth century. Around 1910, her first translation into German appears, the Swedish children's book *The Funny Ways of the Mushroom People,* with illustrations by Signe Aspeling.[13] A second translation follows three years later, this time from English to German. The edition *Lamb's Rendition of Shakespeare's Tales* contains prose narratives arranged for children and teenagers based on famous Shakespearean dramas; this book as well is complemented by illustrations, here by Arthur Schreiner.[14]

---

13 *Des Pilzlingsvolkes lustig' Treiben Will ich in Bild und Wort beschreiben.* See bibliography for full citation.
14 *Shakespeare Erzählungen nach Lamb.* See bibliography for full citation.

The translations are evidence of Else Dormitzer's attempts to enter the ever-growing market of children's and young adult books in Imperial Germany. Until the early 1930s, she writes and publishes at least twenty-nine original children's books using her pseudonym Else Dorn. She also contributes six original stories and fairy tales to anthologies, among them, for example, the Christmas tale "What the Christmas Trees Tell Each Other" for the collection *For the Hour of Dusk: New Fairy Tales and Stories* by Elisabeth Dauthendey or the Easter story *To the Well-Behaved Child from the Easter Bunny*.[15]

Most of her publications are picture and cardboard books for children, published by the Löwensohn Publishing House in Fürth and the Pestalozzi Publishing Firm in Berlin, a company bought by Löwensohn at the end of the 1920s. These short books contain stories and scenes from the animal world along with adventure, travel, and vacation stories, mostly in verse form with simple rhymes and accompanied by colored illustrations. Titles like *Funny Stories from the Countryside, Vacation at the Seashore,* or *Let's Go on a Trip around the World!* suggest the representation of an idyllic and idealized world for children, in which boys and girls live carefree lives, travel magically to far-away places, and find harmony with animals and the natural world.[16]

Targeted to reach a broad audience, they do not promote the active, new child of progressive education or question bourgeois morals and values but rather affirm them. Parents cherish and reward well-behaved, good children, whereas they discipline naughty ones, raising them to be hard-working adults and responsible citizens of society, as one can read on the opening pages of what probably is Dormitzer's first children's book *How Diligent Children Spend Their Time* (1900): "Listen, lovely children, let us be like bees! Work diligently, late and early, and don't shy away from any kind of struggle. Then later in life, you will be nothing but efficient people!"[17]

With the introduction of the so-called Law of Association (*Reichsvereinsgesetz*) on May 15, 1908, a national law permitting women official membership in political unions and organizations, Else also starts increasing her public service commitments and engagements outside the

---

15 *Für die Dämmerstunde, Neue Märchen und Geschichten,* "Was sich die Weihnachtsbäume erzählen," *Dem braven Kind vom Osterhas.* See bibliography for full citation.
16 *Lustiges vom Land, Auf zur Weltreise, Ferien an der See.* See bibliography for full citation.
17 *Wie fleißige Kinder die Zeit sich vertreiben Mit Kochen und Waschen, mit Lesen und Schreiben.* See bibliography for full citation.

home. She already showed her talent for organization by supporting the charity work of the local Nuremberg congregation, contributing greatly to the preservation of unity and spirit of the Jewish community. Now, however, she can actively support organizations that are of primary importance to her in newfound ways. Next to the Aid Organization of German Jews, an organization also supported by her husband, she dedicates her time to the newly created Association for Liberal Judaism in Germany (1908), of which Nuremberg Rabbi Dr. Max Freudenthal (1868–1937) is a founding and board member. Dormitzer also submits articles for publication in the association's monthly magazine *Liberal Judaism* and the weekly *Jewish-Liberal Newspaper* and, additionally starts giving public lectures.[18]

Her written and spoken contributions mirror the organization's basic principles, a self-confident Reform Judaism paying particular attention to the "stronger participation of women in religious and community life."[19] In February 1914, she delivers a "captivating and poised" lecture entitled "Questions about Jewish Daily Life" at the association's local branch in Nuremberg, according to a review in the *General Newspaper of Judaism*, resulting in "enthusiastic applause and recognition" from the audience.[20] Demanding a proud affirmation of Judaism, she illustrates the necessity of a modern-day religious education, one that should include not only biblical history but also the cultural, political, and economic contributions of German Jews to German society at large. The goal of such an education, the review quotes Dormitzer, "should not only be that children will be made conscious of Judaism's value but also that they will be truthful to the faith of their fathers with understanding reverence."

World War I and the Weimar Republic, 1914–1933

During World War I (1914–1918), Else Dormitzer starts expanding her advocacy work in yet another organization, the Central Union of German Citizens of Jewish Faith, which organizes spring and fall membership drives for women following the introduction of the Law of Association in early 1908. Founded in Berlin on March 28, 1893, as a national organization to

---

18 *Liberales Judentum: Monatsschrift für die religiösen Interessen des Judentums, Jüdisch-Liberale Zeitung.*
19 "Program," *Liberales Judentum* 1 (1908): 17.
20 "Der Gemeindebote," supplement, *Allgemeine Zeitung des Judentums*, February 27, 1914.

fight and end antisemitism in German society and politics, the Central Union now sees the potential of recruiting women as new members and supporters for their cause.[21] On November 24, 1908, the scope of this work is presented during the Union's first women's assembly meeting in Berlin:

> The women would see their main task as supporting the men in their fight against a movement adverse to culture; she would encourage him, keep him from discouragement, educate their children to be striking personalities, equip them early on with religious doctrine, and render children resistant to ridicule and affront and to protect the youth of cowardly renunciation; to bring up all Jews with pride [...].[22]

It is within this context of the anticipated role for female members that her service to the Central Union and the Union for Liberal Judaism during and after World War I needs to be understood. Dormitzer is not questioning or denying the traditional role of the Jewish woman as mother, wife, housewife, and keeper of religion. She does, however, see herself as an equal partner, as someone who contributes independently to the success of the organizations through her own thinking and, most of all, doing. She certainly does not wish to be relegated to the sidelines and play a merely passive, supporting role in advocating for liberal Judaism or in countering an increasingly aggressive antisemitism.

Inspired by the success of the women's movement, particularly The League of Jewish Women headed by Bertha Pappenheim, she envisions going beyond the scope set for women by the Central Union in 1908, whose board wants women to be members but not leaders.[23] Advocating confidently and directly for her goals, she identifies the need for women to be recognized as equal contributors to the cause, assisting "particularly with actions," as she writes in her 1917 article "The Jewish Woman in Propaganda." "It is simply not enough that we tend to the idea, which we identified as right, behind closed doors, but we need to champion it in spoken and in written word, and

---

21 Avraham Barkai, "*Wehr Dich!*" Der Centralverein deutscher Staatsbürger jüdischen Glaubens *1893–1938* (Munich: C. H. Beck, 2002).

22 Else Dormitzer, "Vereinsnachrichten," *Im Deutschen Reich. Zeitschrift des Centralvereins Deutscher Staatsbürger Jüdischen Glaubens* 12 (1908): 719.

23 Kaplan, *The Making of the Jewish Middle Class*, 69.

we must especially succeed in clearly convincing all those who do not think like us."[24] Her self-confidence and commitment when publicly representing the interests of these organizations, in particular, that of the Central Union after 1917, as well as her ideas about improving the visibility and effectiveness of its work, over time, no longer align with the priorities of the Central Union and clash with the predominantly male board. This, in turn, leads to tensions in the 1920s on the regional and national level and, finally, by 1928, to a reduction of her work for the organization.

Strengthened by the women's right to vote after the end of World War I, Else Dormitzer's publications, except for her children's books, now become more politically and socially engaged, increasingly focusing on the role of women in society and religion. The opportunity for women to vote and to be elected to office, she argues in her 1919 essay "The Demands of the Jewish Woman" for *Liberal Judaism*, should serve as a model for congregations. Finally, women can become valued, equal partners by taking on previously denied roles in local Jewish communities.

> What do we demand? We demand active participation in all matters of Jewish community life—not only in the areas of charity work or caretaking, which women already engage in everywhere, but also the right to vote and to representation in all other areas of community life, particularly in administration, which until now has only been possible for men. Why should women, who pursue the same interests as men, who care just as much for the wellbeing of their community, not serve as advisors for general affairs? Why should women not give counsel in religious matters if laymen can even partake in these affairs at all?[25]

She assumes that this change will not happen without a fight or concerted effort since all kinds of prejudice will need to be eliminated along the way. In her own congregation, however, these words resonate loud and clearly and, in 1922, Else Dormitzer is elected to the administrative board of her

---

24 Else Dormitzer, "Die jüdische Frau in der Propaganda," *Liberales Judentum* 5–6 (1917): 66–68.
25 Else Dormitzer, "Die Forderung der jüdischen Frau," *Liberales Judentum* 3–4 (1919): 26–28.

congregation in Nuremberg, making her not only the first woman in Bavaria but in all of Germany in such a position.[26] From now on, she is officially engaged in the day-to-day work of the local Jewish community. Despite these new opportunities for women, Else Dormitzer and Paula Erlanger remain the only two elected female representatives until the 1930s out of a total of twenty-seven members.[27]

Before her election to the board, however, she approaches Rabbi Freudenthal in the fall of 1920 with the suggestion of starting a monthly newsletter to facilitate communication between the congregation and its members.[28] In favor of this proposal, Dr. Freudenthal supports her efforts, and beginning in 1921, the *Nuremberg Israelite Community Paper* appears monthly until it ceases production in 1938.[29] After encountering financial difficulties at the start, caused mainly by the hyperinflation of 1923, the editorial committee succeeds in establishing the newsletter and making it an integral part of the Nuremberg Jewish community. Else Dormitzer contributes significantly to the success of this project. Starting in 1926, the Jewish Community in Fürth also becomes part of the newsletter, from then on, appearing as the *Nuremberg-Fürth Israelite Community Paper*.[30] The editors not only publish community news and announcements of interest to congregants but also include a range of cultural, religious, and political contributions, such as reviews of local cultural programs, religious reflections, or assessments of political events.

During her work as editor, Else also contributes several pieces, including a travel report of a visit to the synagogue in Rome (April 1925) and a review of Ernst Feder's biography on the founder of the Aid Organization of German Jews, Paul Nathan (January 1929).[31] In the column "On Literature," she also regularly shares book recommendations.[32] Even though she is still

---

26 Rosenberg, *Spuren und Fragmente*, 127.

27 "Aus der Gemeindestube," *Nürnberger Israelitisches Gemeindeblatt* 8, no. 5 (January 1928): 83.

28 Else Dormitzer, "Dem Redaktionskollegen des Nürnberger-Fürther Gemeindeblatts," *Nürnberger-Fürther Israelitisches Gemeindeblatt* 11, no. 1 (March 1931): 111.

29 *Nürnberger Israelitisches Gemeindeblatt*.

30 *Nürnberger-Fürther Israelitisches Gemeindeblatt*.

31 Else Dormitzer, "Ein Freitagabend in der Hauptsynagoge zu Rom," *Nürnberger Israelitisches Gemeindeblatt* 5, no. 11–12 (July–August 1925): 92–93. Else Dormitzer, "Paul Nathan. Ein Lebensbild von Ernst Feder," *Nürnberger-Fürther Israelitisches Gemeindeblatt* 9, no. 5 (January 1929): 91–92.

32 "Literarisches."

on the congregation's administrative board by 1937, her work for the newsletter becomes less frequent in the 1930s. The 1933 March edition probably contains her last article, a review of a public program organized by the *Jewish-Liberal Newspaper* in the heart of Berlin on January 30, the day German President Paul von Hindenburg names Adolf Hitler chancellor of Germany.[33]

> With exaltation, one stepped out into the cold winter evening after this unique experience [the public program]. In the distance, one could hear the national socialist flush of victory; the swastikas fluttered in the torchlight, the hustle and bustle prevailed in the government district. But the stars still went about their way in the sky. Upon seeing them, one silently repeated the optimistic final word of the evening: We were, we are, we will be.

Parallel to her work on the administrative and editorial boards of the Nuremberg congregation, she tirelessly helps advancing the mission of the Central Union in the 1920s. Triggered by the events of World War I, her first publication for the Central Union appears as early as 1917. A majority of German Jews views the beginning of war in 1914 as an unprecedented opportunity of proving their love for the German nation, and organizations like the Central Union issue calls to voluntarily take up arms in defense of the fatherland.[34] However, already at the end of 1914, the national antisemitic organization *Reichshammerbund*, part of an extensive network of right-wing groups and organizations in Imperial Germany, starts spreading rumors that "German Jews lack patriotic engagement and willingness to make sacrifices."[35]

In 1916, the German military conducts a census of Jewish war participation, the so-called Statistical Survey about Employment Contracts of German Jews in the War, a slap in the face for Jewish soldiers giving their lives for their homeland on the front lines.[36] They watch in bewilderment how their own government, too, buys into the unfounded antisemitic lies of them only feigning their loyalty to the German nation, being traitors to the cause. With the German war effort at home and abroad increasingly failing,

33 Else Dormitzer, "Männer der Feder sprechen," *Nürnberger-Fürther Israelitisches Gemeindeblatt* 13, no. 1 (March 1933): 3.
34 Hecht, *Deutsche Juden und Antisemitismus*, 55ff.
35 Ibid., 57.
36 *Statistische Erhebung über die Dienstverhältnisse der deutschen Juden im Krieg.*

it seems as if most of the population is soon forgetting the words of German Emperor Wilhelm II, who, at the beginning of the war, stated that he no longer knew political parties but only Germans. Intent on preserving internal peace, Jewish organizations like the Central Union have heeded the *Kaiser's* call for a unified home front, and consequently stopped their defense work. As a consequence, the antisemitic accusations of the survey further contribute to German Jews losing their faith of ever being fully recognized by society and the government as equals—and as Germans.[37]

Else Dormitzer directly addresses the military census in her 1917 article "Experiences from my Advocacy Activities" in the Central Union's publication *In the German Reich* and, in plain language, cautions readers of a deteriorating situation after the end of the war:

> We only need to pronounce this evil phrase, "Jew Census," words that are heart-wrenching to us, to garner sympathy and approval. The outrage about these dreadful statistics upsets every Jew, pushing blood into our cheeks. And it will take a long time for all to swallow this bitter pill; for those on the front and those at home. Just noting the ability of the Central Union in their fight against the census and their defense against other kinds of hostility is getting us new members. But even the optimists among us have surrendered the belief that the emperor's words, "I no longer know political parties; I only know Germans," should practically include us Jews. That the sacrifices we Jews made for this war and are still making in goods and with our blood will silence those spiteful voices who still want to see us as alien. Antisemitic maliciousness is venturing out against us in the most shameless fashion, even in plain view of this truce. It is now up to us to prepare ourselves for the worsening of times that will start after the war.[38]

Thus, World War I does not integrate German Jews more into society as they have hoped just a few years earlier but rather isolates them further, even if the Weimar Constitution now grants equality by law.

---

37 Hecht, *Deutsche Juden und Antisemitismus*, 56.
38 Else Dormitzer, "Erfahrungen aus meiner Werbetätigkeit," *Im deutschen Reich* 3 (March 1917): 121–123.

Among the antisemitic images frequently being used are that of the "Jewish slacker" and the "Jewish winner of the war," responsible for and profiting from Germany's post-war economic misery. Antisemitism in all areas of society increases during the years of the Weimar Republic, including organized public assaults against German Jews. The city of Nuremberg itself becomes important in the struggle of the right for power, of which the National Socialist German Workers Party (NSDAP) under the leadership of Adolf Hitler ultimately emerges victorious.[39]

Julius Streicher establishes the local group of the National Socialists in Nuremberg in October 1922, six months before he begins spreading his antisemitic tirades in his weekly newspaper *Der Stürmer*, including against members of Nuremberg's Jewish community.[40] Under the watchful eyes of Streicher, Hitler as well as other party and state delegates, including Prince Ludwig Ferdinand of Bavaria, Nuremberg hosts its first "German Day" in September 1923, bringing together different regional right-wing groups and organizations in a display of unity only weeks before the failed Nazi attempt to overthrow the government in the "Beer Hall Putsch" in Munich. The early success of the "German Day," with its grand parade on Nuremberg's main square, the *Hauptmarkt*, and the show of armed forces in the *Luitpoldhain*, serves Hitler as a model for the Nazi Party rallies held annually in Nuremberg after 1933.[41]

Ten years before the Third Reich becomes a reality, the German-Jewish press in particular, views the year 1923 as one of crisis: pogrom-like riots directed at Jewish institutions and civilians break out in several cities across Germany, and such attacks are no longer just targeting public figures.[42] Triggered by antisemitic lies in *Der Stürmer*, the Nuremberg Jewish Congregation is fearing attacks on its synagogue in the spring of 1923. On November 6 of the same year, the *Jewish Review* reports on several attacks against German Jews in Nuremberg:

---

39 Rainer Hambrecht illustrates the importance of Nuremberg and other parts of Franconia in the early history of the National Socialists' struggle to consolidate power in his study *Die Braune Bastion. Der Aufstieg der NSDAP in Mittel-und Oberfranken (1922–1933)* (Petersberg: Michael Imhof, 2017).

40 Melanie Wager, "Warenhausjude, Wäschejude, Autojude. *Der Stürmer* und die Arisierung," in *Entrechtet. Entwürdigt. Beraubt. Die Arisierung in Nürnberg und Fürth*, ed. Matthias Henkel and Eckart Dietzfelbinger (Petersberg: Michael Imhof, 2012), 17–39.

41 Hambrecht, *Die Braune Bastion*, 50–54.

42 Hecht, *Deutsche Juden und Antisemitismus*, 173ff.

National Socialists youth groups assaulted Jewish pedestrians and wounded several of them badly. On his way home, a well-known lawyer was injured so severely that he had to be carried away unconsciously. Three Jewish merchants were stabbed with knives and wounded, not harmlessly, in this manner. Groups of rioters entered the apartments of Jewish citizens by force and searched their homes. Windows of Jewish restaurants were destroyed. Posters around town called for "the killing of Jews like dogs." The whole situation is heightened by the fact that the Nuremberg police is not under the authority of the democratic mayor but is closely entangled with the National Socialists. The Nuremberg city council assembled and spoke out in unison against these attacks, launching serious charges against the police and the justice administration.[43]

One month before the murder in June 1922 of German foreign minister Walther Rathenau, one of the most prominent German Jews in public life, Else Dormitzer publishes her article "The Woman and the Central Union" in the first edition of the *Central Union Newspaper*, calling on her female readers to step up their work for the organization in light of the clear and present danger. It is up to women, she writes, to actively support the men in their defense activities. Women should not wait until the "atmosphere of pogroms is knocking on their own door" but become engaged immediately. This could happen in a few ways, for example, by becoming a member of the Union and encouraging others to do the same or by participating in acts of daily resistance—in school, on the streets, in stores. Women, she writes, should intervene, not stand by, or watch in silence.

> Hasn't every Jewish mother witnessed an antisemitic experience of their child in school? Hasn't she grieved and felt outraged about the hatred and the resets experienced by her sons and daughters? And, honestly, has anyone here picked up the gauntlet without thinking twice, demanding her rights and receiving them? There is no hesitation, no standing back—wherever there is an antisemitic advance, it needs to

---

43 "Antisemitische Exzesse in Deutschland," *Jüdische Rundschau*, November 6, 1923.

be countered. Women and mothers need to bravely step up and put an end to it.[44]

At the time of the Nuremberg riots on November 6, 1923, Else Dormitzer is part of the board of both the local and regional branches of the Central Union. Elected to the organization's national committee in 1919, she is serving alongside two other women, Dr. Cora Berliner and Henriette May, the latter also essential in the creation of The League of Jewish Women in 1904.[45] The formation of new women's groups in the fight against antisemitism is of particular interest to Dormitzer, as she highlights in a letter to the Central Union's leadership in 1925. Nuremberg, she writes, was one of the first cities in which women's assemblies were established, stating, "for years our local branch has been organizing one or two meetings every winter for women with female presenters."[46]

After attending the organization's national meetings, she enjoys the opportunity of giving talks to female audiences in Berlin and its surrounding areas. Dr. Ludwig Holländer, director of the Central Union and principal editor of its newspaper since 1922, is relying on her experience in setting up these groups and further solicits her help. She engages in steady correspondence with him and other national representatives between 1922 and 1928, and Holländer actively supports Dormitzer's advocacy work by arranging public lectures for her. After falling ill in September 1922, for example, his secretary Miss Stern inquires on Holländer's behalf if she could take his place in presenting a lecture in the Baden region of Southwest Germany, an invitation, Dormitzer declines because of prior commitments and time constraints.[47]

In the winter months of 1925, she goes on a lecture tour across the country, giving twenty presentations in different locations. She does so voluntarily and without compensation. Lectures like "Onslaught and Resistance" (1922), "National—Much Too National" (1925), and "The German Jewish Woman in German Folk Life" (1926) further contribute to the educational

---

44 Else Dormitzer, "Die Frau und der Centralverein," *CV-Zeitung*, May 4, 1922.
45 Rebekka Denz, *Bürgerlich, Jüdisch, Weiblich. Frauen im Centralverein deutscher Staatsbürger Jüdischen Glaubens* (Berlin: Neofelis, 2022), 40.
46 Correspondence Else Dormitzer with Miss Stern, January 17, 1925, and January 19, 1915, Document 55/39/1608, Wiener Holocaust Library.
47 Correspondence Else Dormitzer, September 29, 1922, and October 4, 1922, Document 55/39/1608, Wiener Holocaust Library.

mission of the Central Union. After her lecture tours, the administrative board in Berlin requests travel reports, and Dormitzer not only writes in detail about her presentations and their reception (e.g. number of audience participants, the quality of the Q&A, and the discussion in general) but also includes assessments of the efficiency of individual local and regional branch organizations. These reports are often quite critical, and she sends them directly to the offices of Dr. Holländer and Dr. Alfred Wiener, deputy director of the Central Union between 1923 and 1933.

At the request of The League of Jewish Women, Dormitzer also goes on a lecture tour through the state of Hesse in February 1926 to support the group's "Week of the Women's Vote." Presumably, Else Dormitzer is a member of The League of Jewish Women since her views on women's participation in Jewish communities align with their goals. Moreover, the group is also linked organizationally with the Central Union, as Rebekka Denz illustrates in her study of women in the organization, resulting in the joining of the Central Union women's groups with The League of Jewish Women in 1928.[48] Not surprisingly, Dormitzer's 1925 essay *Famous Jewish Women in Past and Present*, published as a brochure for the Central Union and based on one of her previous talks, praises the League's strong female leadership.

> No less excellent are the contemporary leaders of the women's movement, whose names will be listed only to illustrate their brilliant accomplishments: Bertha Pappenheim, the previous chairwoman of the The League of Jewish Women, the founder of the well-known social home in Neu-Isenburg, who also was active as a writer; Henriette May, Sidonie Werner, Henriette Fürth; the actions of all these women are dedicated to the Jewish women's movement and their exemplary achievements in the areas of philanthropy, the sciences and the development of all educational branches.[49]

Illustrating the accomplishments of Jewish women in German culture from past to present—from Glückel von Hameln to Else Lasker-Schüler—the

---

48 Denz, *Bürgerlich, Jüdisch, Weiblich*, 289.
49 Else Dormitzer, *Berühmte Jüdische Frauen in Vergangenheit und Gegenwart* (Berlin: Philo, 1925), 19.

essay's goal is to "destroy the fairy tale of the inferiority of the Jews."[50] These women should serve as models for inspiration and imitation for contemporaries. Since some Jewish communities still do not allow women to vote in community matters, Dormitzer also directly addresses her readers, asking them to take it upon themselves to correct this situation.

Famous Jewish Women in Past and Present is a passionate plea for women's equality; it is primarily women who have "contributed to the perfection and refinement of humankind."[51] With the cost of fifty cents a copy, Dormitzer instructs for the royalties to go directly into a foundation fund managed by the Central Union. Published by the Philo-Verlag, a press belonging to the Central Union, the essay proves particularly successful and is already in its third edition by 1927. Appearing in the series "The Light," the brochure is actively used for educational work; for example, at the Union's behest, individual brochures are distributed in public places for easy access and wide circulation.[52]

The Third Reich, 1933–1939

After increasing disagreements with the Bavarian regional branch of the Central Union, Else Dormitzer starts reducing her local work in the organization in 1928, focusing her energy instead on serving the Nuremberg congregation in various ways. The newsletter's editorial team and the Jewish community's administrative board continue to benefit from her expertise. In 1927, a total of thirteen children's books appears in the Pestalozzi Publishing House in Berlin, and her journalistic pieces continue to be printed in magazines and newspapers like the *Berlin Daily Newspaper.* Whenever possible, she also continues to lend support by advocating for the work of the crematoria associations.

It is only after 1933 and after the beginning of the exclusion of German Jews from all areas of public life that her output decreases.

> From the outset, the Nazi government used legislation, administrative decrees, and propaganda to defame and ostracize Jews and to lower their social, economic, and legal standing. The April Boycott of 1933 attempted to expose German

---

50   Ibid., introduction, iii.
51   Ibid., 5.
52   Hecht, *Deutsche Juden und Antisemitismus*, 128–129.

Jews to public opprobrium and to destroy Jewish businesses, and the laws of that month limited Jewish participation in the economy. In September 1935, the Nuremberg Laws formally deprived Jews of their rights as citizens and established racial segregation. It took less than two years to destroy the foundation upon which Jewish life had existed in Germany since the country's unification in 1871.[53]

In 1930, 414,000 inhabitants call the city of Nuremberg their home; 2,4% of these citizens are Jewish; in all of Germany, it is 0.77% of the total population, about half a million people.[54] A few days after the national book burnings on May 10, 1933, in twenty cities across Germany, an event organized by the German Student Union (*Deutsche Studentenschaft*) to cleanse society of its "degenerate," "un-German" spirit, Else Dormitzer publishes an article in the *Jewish-Liberal Newspaper*, urgently calling on Jewish women to reflect on their roles and to set aside their own desires and needs considering the incredibly difficult times: "Companion to her husband, adviser to her children, servant to the general public, this is how she stands in front of us, the Jewish woman."[55] When after twenty-five years of voluntary, uncompensated work for the Economic Union of Nuremberg Artists, Sigmund Dormitzer is barred from his post in March 1933, only one artist has the courage "to thank him publicly for what he had achieved for the arts and artists of Nuremberg."[56] With limitations, he is allowed to practice law until November 1938; the Nuremberg Bar Association, however, no longer grants the same permission to Hildegard, who completes her law degree *magna cum laude* in 1933.[57]

---

53 Marion A. Kaplan, *Between Dignity and Despair: Jewish Life in Nazi Germany* (Oxford: Oxford University Press, 1998), 17.

54 Kolb, *Die Juden in Nürnberg 1839–1945*, 11–12. Also see Bundeszentrale für politische Bildung, "Vertreibung und Deportation der Juden aus dem Deutschen Reich," accessed December 2, 2022, https://www.bpb.de/fsd/centropa/judenindeutschland 1933_1939.php.

55 Else Dormitzer, "Die Kameradin des Mannes," supplement, *Jüdisch-Liberale Zeitung*, May 15, 1933.

56 Rosenberg, *Spuren und Fragmente*, 127.

57 Reinhard Weber, "Berufliche Ausgrenzung von jüdischen Rechtsanwälten und Justizbediensteten," in *Entrechtet. Entwürdigt. Beraubt. Die Arisierung in Nürnberg und Fürth*, ed. Matthias Henkel and Eckart Dietzfelbinger (Petersberg: Michael Imhof, 2012), 83–89. "Secret and public boycotts by government agencies and the business world limited the economic scope of many lawyers and allowed the steady displacement of Jews

The Dormitzers now witness the city's architectural reconfiguration for the annual *NSDAP* rallies and its instrumentalization for the Nazi cause. Located south-east of the city, at a World War I memorial site dedicated to fallen German soldiers, the extensive rally grounds become home to five massive structures, among them the never completed Congress Hall—inspired by the Colosseum in Rome—and the Zeppelin Field, which can accommodate up to 240,000 rally participants.[58] Modeled after the Pergamon Altar, its northern tribune is a "long grandstand-like structure, flanked at each end with massive 'book end' pylons, and dignified by a colonnaded screen behind the seating, topped by a giant swastika set in an oak-leaf wreath," further exemplifying National Socialist fascination with bombastic form and neoclassical style inscribed with its own symbolism.[59] But, as Joshua Hagen and Robert Ostergren illustrate, the focus in Nuremberg does not solely rest on the erection of new structures for the annual staging of a united, idealized *völkisch* community gathered around its supreme leader but also on the restoration and renovation of the city's old town.[60]

> Although seemingly irreconcilable in terms of style and scale, these efforts to build and rebuild in Nuremberg were actually seen as complementing elements in the regime's programme to create and project images of historical greatness, current political legitimacy and promises of future grandeur. […] Nazi party officials embarked on a purposeful program to adapt Nuremberg's city centre to a specific version of history that would buttress the Nazi Party's political authority

---

from the profession even without legal grounds. Until 1938, 98 lawyers relinquished their rights to practice law. Of 440 Bavarian Jewish lawyers in 1933, only 266 were still working in 1935. In the fall of 1938, the number was 175. Ultimately, the fifth amendment to the Reich Citizenship Law decreed the final ban for all remaining lawyers to be implemented by November 30, 1938" (ibid., 86).

58 "The Nazi Party Rally Grounds," Documentation Center Nazi Party Rally Grounds— The Nuremberg Municipal Museums, accessed May 19, 2022, https://museums. nuernberg.de/documentation-center/the-site/the-nazi-party-rally-grounds/information-system-rally-grounds/point-08. For more information on the party rally grounds at Nuremberg see Paul Jaskot, *The Architecture of Oppression: The SS, Forced Labor and the Nazi Monumental Building Economy* (London: Taylor & Francis Group, 1999).

59 Joshua Hagen and Robert Ostergren, "Spectacle, Architecture and Place at the Nuremberg Party Rallies: Projecting a Nazi Vision of Past, Present and Future," *Cultural Geographies* 13, no. 2 (2006): 160–161.

60 Ibid., 157–181.

and its self-image as chief steward and pinnacle of German cultural and historical greatness. These efforts led by Mayor Willy Liebel, were implemented by a small cadre of professional architects, preservationists, and urban planners sympathetic to the regime's apparent commitment to preserving and restoring Germany's historical monuments.[61]

As part of this project, the city government orders to tear down the main synagogue in the summer of 1938, according to the words of Mayor Liebel, "the greatest architectural sin of the last decades."

> One of the most regrettable chapters of the architectural history of Nuremberg of the last century will come to an end with the successful removal of the synagogue: the "disgrace of Nuremberg" will be redeemed by the removal of this oriental structure that, as *Der Stürmer* only recently and so very rightly observed, "rises ostentatiously, soullessly, and brazenly above the sea of houses of Nuremberg."[62]

On August 10, 1938—three months before the nationwide destruction of synagogues during the state-sponsored November attacks—a large crowd of civilians joins Liebel, Julius Streicher, members of the SA (*Sturmabteilung/* Storm Troopers or Brownshirts) as well as other Nazi officials on *Spitalplatz* for the public spectacle.[63] After several speeches, a group of construction workers begins demolition of the synagogue by removing its dome and two entry candelabras. "Those in the demolition crew who were watching on

---

61 Ibid., 157 and 166–167.

62 Kolb, *Die Juden in Nürnberg 1839–1945*, 52–53. Nuremberg had two synagogues: the main synagogue on *Spitalplatz* in the city center (1874) and the synagogue on *Essenweinstraße 7* (1902). Home to the Orthodox community, the latter was destroyed in November 1938. Also see Cornelia Berger-Dittscheid, "Zwischen Reform und Tradition—die Synagogen des 19. und 20. Jahrhunderts in Nürnberg," in *Geschichte und Kultur der Juden in Nürnberg*, ed. Andrea M. Kluxen and Julia Krieger (Würzburg: Ergon, 2014), 213–245.

63 See the introduction (footnote 14) for further discussion of the terminology used to describe the anti-Jewish terror of November 9 and 10, 1938.

raised their right arm for the Hitler salute."[64] Later, the spectators cheer on Streicher as he and other officials leave the square in a car convoy.

Needing to make constant changes due to the ever-growing, restrictive legal decrees by the government, Else Dormitzer stands by her community during this difficult time. Jewish communities and organizations soon become the sole points of contact for persecuted citizens wishing to receive counsel or help.[65] After the creation of the Jewish Cultural Union in Bavaria in 1934, she tries to aid its establishment in Nuremberg. From now on, all religious, scientific, and artistic events need to be organized under the auspices of the Jewish Cultural Union.

> The Jewish Cultural Union offered entertainment to Jewish audiences, employed Jewish artists who had been fired as a result of racial decrees, and provided a semblance of leisure for its almost 70,000 members in forty-nine locals. Of course, the Nazi regime permitted the Union solely for its own advantage, to hide the oppression of Jews. Moreover, the Union could not perform works forbidden by the Nazis: at first, for example, Germanic legends, and, later, the works of Schiller, Goethe, Beethoven, or Wagner.[66]

In Nuremberg, Else Dormitzer is lending a helping hand by organizing musical hours for Jewish youth. Starting in the summer of 1937, the Union's local event announcements are published in the congregation's newsletter until its publication ceases in 1938. Following directives from the government's Ministry of Enlightenment and Propaganda headed by Joseph Goebbels, the newsletter is earlier renamed *Jewish Community Newsletter for the Israelite Communities of Nuremberg and Fürth*. Elisabeth Rosenfelder, a trained singer, performs in such a concert organized by the Jewish Cultural Union on January 18, 1937. A few months earlier, her husband Ernst and his business partners Gustav and Robert Löwensohn receive an ultimatum

---

64 Alexander Schmidt, "Scheinbare Normalität: "Drei Skizzen zur Geschichte der Nürnberger Juden 1918 bis 1938," in *Geschichte und Kultur der Juden in Nürnberg*, ed. Andrea M. Kluxen and Julia Krieger (Würzburg: Ergon, 2014), 304.

65 Yaakov Barut, "Jüdisches Leben in Franken während des Nationalsozialismus," in *Die Juden in Franken*, ed. Michael Brenner and Daniela F. Eisenstein (Munich: Oldenbourg, 2012), 222.

66 Kaplan, *Between Dignity and Despair: Jewish Life in Nazi Germany*, 46–47.

from the government to end their publishing and bookselling operations by December 1937. After the forced sale of their company, the Rosenfelder family decides to leave Germany for the United Kingdom in search of a home abroad. At this point, Hildegard has already emigrated to the Netherlands, as Else Dormitzer recalls in her eyewitness account after the war.

> My younger daughter studied law and completed her state exam at the Nuremberg Palace of Justice on January 4, 1933, at a time when my husband was no longer allowed to enter the building. However, he was re-admitted later on. In August 1933, H. received the title of Assessor, after she had previously completed her doctorate in law *magna cum laude*. Of course, she was barred from practicing law, of any kind, in Germany and therefore went to Prague in October 1933, where she learned Czech and worked for an accountant. Since it was not possible for her to advance her career in Czechoslovakia, she did not stay there long. She married a man from Aachen, who was half-Jewish and whom she met while studying in Munich. The two of them emigrated to Holland in the year 1937 and lived in Hilversum, until the end of the war. My older daughter E. and her husband and children found the right moment to leave and emigrated to England.[67]

The daughters repeatedly insist on the emigration of their parents but to no avail; Else and Sigmund do not want to leave their hometown and burden their children abroad. It is only after the anti-Jewish state terror in November 1938 during which Sigmund Dormitzer is severely wounded and much of the family apartment in *Blumenstraße* destroyed that the children succeed in convincing them of the necessity. "I ask father and you to join us in Hilversum," writes Richard Haas on November 12 to his mother-in-law. "We have already completed the preliminary steps for your entry into Holland, and it would be a great relief to us if you would grant us our wish and we succeed in securing the residence permit." Twice, Else Dormitzer states in her post-war report, fifteen *SA* men intrude on their home, ravaging it and wounding her husband severely.

---

67   Else Dormitzer, "Experiences." See introduction, footnote 3.

That night, we were assaulted twice in our home: First came about fifteen *SA* men who abused and injured us severely; they smashed the furniture in our apartment, cut the pillows and furniture to pieces and behaved like vandals. Later, more thugs appeared, invaded our bedroom, and broke my husband's nose with a steel rod. They abused us both barbarically. After this attack we were driven into the street, drenched in blood, and went to see a Christian doctor nearby. We did not know him, and it seemed that he did not comprehend fully what was happening, since he thought he could call the riot squad for help. Yet he behaved in an extremely humane and sympathetic way towards us. At three in the morning, we took a taxi to the Jewish Hospital in Fürth, where we were admitted.[68]

On the third day of his hospital stay and after pressure from the relevant government offices, she and her husband agree to the forced sale of their home in *Blumenstraße*. House and property have a value of 150,000 Reichsmark (RM), however, they must sell it to the government for 10,000 RM. The way in which government expropriations under the guise of Aryanization play out in Nuremberg is particularly corrupt: A nationwide scandal ensues since large sums of these "sales" do not land in the pockets of the Reich, as intended, but in the private hands of local politicians. With help from Reich Marshal Hermann Göring, the president of the police of Nuremberg-Fürth, Dr. Benno Martin, and Mayor Willy Liebel succeed during the official investigations in depriving District Leader Julius Streicher of his power. Julius Streicher is one of the main culprits in the so-called *Holzaktion*, named after another corrupt local *NSDAP* actor in the expropriations, Karl Holz.[69] Göring puts in place a committee to investigate and revise the illegal Aryanizations, and afterward, a small sum of the forced sale goes to the Dormitzers, who, at this point, have already fled to the Netherlands. Of course, the German politics of Aryanization do not change. However, after the experience in Nuremberg,

---

68 Ibid.
69 See also Thomas Auburger, "Die Staatspolizeistelle Nürnberg-Fürth," in *Entrechtet. Entwürdigt. Beraubt. Die Arisierung in Nürnberg und Fürth*, ed. Matthias Henkel und Eckart Dietzfelbinger (Petersberg: Michael Imhof, 2012), 113–121; and also the article by Matthias Klaus Braun in the same volume, "Die Stadtverwaltung Nürnberg und ihre Beteiligung an der Arisierung," 123–137.

the National Socialists make sure that the Reich and the finance ministry profit from the revenue—and not greedy individuals. After completion of the forced sale, a government branch office in charge of regional expropriations takes up space in the Dormitzers' home on *Blumenstraße* until 1942, the so-called "Office for the Aryanization for Property at the Commissioner for the De-Judaification of Property in the District of Franconia."

In the winter of 1938/1939, the Dormitzers are busy preparing for their departure. After several weeks of restless waiting, they finally receive the required exit permit from the German Reich. For their immigration, they need not only approval and official paperwork from abroad but also permission from the German government to leave their home country. The daughters watch in trepidation from the United Kingdom and the Netherlands, increasingly on edge about getting their parents to safety and mulling over the necessity of illegal measures in case open doors should close unexpectedly during this volatile, ever-changing situation. In a letter dated January 19, 1939, Hildegard writes her sister in London, reporting on the chaotic situation at government offices in Nuremberg.

> What she tells us about the general conditions and, in particular, how these arrangements unfold is horrible. They all claim that they know nothing of the unlawful acts committed by different offices, for example, the finance ministry claims that the house cannot have been confiscated for the price they received. Apart from their malice, chaos reigns at all offices.

While much of their property was destroyed during the November attack, the Dormitzers need special permission from the finance ministry for all objects they plan on taking abroad. Sigmund is preoccupied with the forced sale settlement of his law firm, and it is his wife who takes care of dissolving the household and organizing their belongings. In January 1939, they temporarily move to *Blumenstraße* 11.[70] Else is in constant contact with friends and relatives who find themselves in a similar position, needing to take care of their own emigration, attempts that are not always successful. On March 1, 1939, the day of departure arrives, and the Dormitzers say their final goodbyes to family and friends. Deprived of their citizenship and robbed of their rights, property, and financial means, they flee their hometown of Nuremberg.

---

70   Registration Card, Else Dormitzer, City Archives Nürnberg, C21/X, Nr.2_263.

CHAPTER THREE

Hilversum and Amsterdam, 1939–1943

The 1938 November pogrom sets off a wave of Jewish refugees from across the German-speaking lands. As a result, the Dutch government departs from its stringent immigration policies and grants a one-time exception for 8,000 Austrian and German Jews to enter the Netherlands. Between 40,000 and 50,000 such requests are initially made.[1] The small neighboring country just west of the German Reich is a popular destination for German-speaking emigrants in the 1930s, admitting approximately 33,000 refugees between 1933 and 1939.[2] While a number of individuals and families arriving in the Netherlands transit to third countries and do not remain within the confines of the Dutch borders, the conservative government led by Prime Minister Hendrik Colijn restricts immigration during these years. On the one hand, the government views the influx in numbers as an additional financial burden during the economic crisis of the 1930s; on the other hand,

> [...] one thought to show consideration of the politically and economically powerful neighbor to the east, the German Reich under national socialist leadership [...] German Jews, who came in illegally, were deported or sent to one of the

---

1 Volker Jakob and Annet van der Vort, *Anne Frank war nicht allein: Lebensgeschichten deutscher Juden in den Niederlanden* (Berlin: Dietz, 1988), 15. Unless otherwise noted, quotes in the main text of this chapter are from documents in the personal archive of surviving family members. Cornelius Partsch translated the three testimonial accounts and poetry collection. All other translations, including secondary materials unavailable in English, are mine.

2 Bob Moore, *Victims and Survivors. The Nazi Persecution of the Jews in the Netherlands* (New York: St. Martin's Press, 1997), 32–33.

Else and Sigmund Dormitzer after their escape to the Netherlands.

newly created internment camps. They could only count on permission to stay if they committed to strict abstinence from political activities and were able to prove that they would not be a financial burden to the Dutch state.[3]

The Dutch public, "fluctuating between the willingness to help and the fear of excessive foreign domination," observes this flow of refugees with mixed feelings.[4] Likewise, social tensions arise between Dutch and German Jews since the government is trying to solve the refugee crisis by transferring its organization to private Jewish aid groups. According to historian Bob Moore, Dutch Jews view their German counterparts as alien, and both minority groups are offended by each other's perceived arrogance, seemingly displaying no other similarities than belonging to the same religion.[5]

---

3   Jakob and van der Vort, *Anne Frank war nicht allein*, 15.
4   Ibid., 13.
5   Moore, *Victims and Survivors*, 31–33.

Three months after arriving in Hilversum, Else and Sigmund Dormitzer travel to the United Kingdom to spend the summer with their daughter, son-in-law, and grandchildren—teenagers by now. Before returning to the Netherlands on August 1, they renew their British visa in London, permitting them a return to the United Kingdom until February 1940. Else is sixty-two years old, her husband just shy of his seventieth birthday on August 14. Having left behind life as they once knew it, they now turn to settling in abroad and adjusting to the new circumstances of living in a foreign country: familiarizing themselves with everyday life, learning a new language, discovering the culture and customs of their host country. They experience financial hardship and rent a room in a boarding house, sharing only a small space. It takes two years after they arrive in the Netherlands to finally receive a small, fixed lump sum from the forced sale of their home in Nuremberg, allowing them, as Sigmund writes in one of his letters, "to support a modest livelihood."[6]

Despite the drastic changes in their lives, the Dormitzers spend the months prior to the German invasion of the Netherlands in May 1940 in relative safety, attempting at least temporarily to recuperate from years of persecution and living in fear. The children take care of them to the best of their abilities, also financially, thanks to their son-in-law's position in the banking sector in Amsterdam. And it does not take long for the Dormitzers to acclimate and appreciate their new surroundings. Eagerly, they immerse themselves in their host country: they learn Dutch, take day trips to Amsterdam and The Hague, visit museums and attend concerts. They also join a congregation where Else readily volunteers her time, suggesting talks for refugees and helping organize the presentations. In a letter to Elisabeth, who is worried about the adjustments her elderly parents are having to make, she writes:

> Do not worry about my lifestyle, it is precisely how I would like it to be, and I feel happiest about it. If I were to just sit around without doing anything at all, then something would be seriously wrong with me. Just wish me the hustle and bustle; there was no lack of it the last few days, but more of that later.

---

6   See footnote 1.

Much of Else's time is dedicated to writing detailed letters to friends, family, and acquaintances, inquiring about their wellbeing, and receiving updated information about their whereabouts, which are, in turn, shared with others in her network. Like his wife, Sigmund also nurtures his contacts through written correspondence, and both practice their language skills by composing letters in English. However, weather permitting, as Sigmund writes in one of them, he prefers going on extended walks.

When World War II breaks out on September 1, 1939, the couple is in complete shock and follows the news attentively for new developments in the days and weeks to come. "Starting at 8:00 a.m. in the morning, we listen to all news and devour our local papers in four languages; it will be the same for you. Our domestic *kranten* are always excellently informed," Else writes in April 1940 to Elisabeth in London. Even though the war worries the family, the couple assesses the situation in the Netherlands as stable and safe, not anticipating a German attack. On the contrary, Sigmund is hopeful that the German invasion of Scandinavia in the spring of 1940 will accelerate the end of the war. As he writes on April 11:

> It is a pleasure to see how calm and trustful people in this country are, especially of course, in this town, where one doesn't observe signs of excitement at all; people are trusting in their strong army and in the possibility to defend the country with means of inundation and so on. In the meantime, spring at last has come, and my daily walks give me more pleasure and satisfaction than ever.[7]

In February of 1940, the family is preoccupied with Hildegard's and Richard's move to their new house in *Graaf Florislaan*. Else helps her daughter with furnishing the rooms, and the parents gift them their curtains from their old apartment on *Blumenstraße* 9, which now adorn the front windows of the Dutch home. Family members, friends, and acquaintances join them for the housewarming party, including Gustav Löwensohn and his wife Emmy, who also escaped Nazi Germany for the Netherlands. Gustav and Emmy present the couple with 300 tulip bulbs for their new garden, which is adorned by a flowering rhododendron bush.

---

7   Quote from Sigmund Dormitzer's original letter, which is in English, not in German.

Around the same time, it appears the Dormitzers are planning to leave the Netherlands for the United Kingdom. There is no hurry, Else writes to Elisabeth on May 1, 1940, "provided there are no unforeseen events, we can definitely stay here for a few more months and take our time in making decisions that the situation requires of us." The impending farewell, she writes five days later, saddens her husband deeply, "he is particularly fond of this land and Hilversum, I would have never thought it possible."

On Friday, May 10, 1940, the German invasion of the Netherlands abruptly upends the Dormitzers' plans, turning their life upside down yet once again. "After the invasion, my husband, like all other Germans, was arrested by the Dutch, but I was able to have him released from internment quickly with the help of a Dutch doctor and a medical attestation," Else writes in her eyewitness account after the war.[8] The swift German offensive leads to the kingdom's unconditional surrender and is signed by Dutch General Henri Winkelman just five days later on May 15. Despite the country's previous capitulation to the *Wehrmacht*, German air strikes reduce the city of Rotterdam to rubble a day earlier, killing approximately 900 people.

While the German forces set up military administrations in other occupied countries in Western Europe, for example, in France and Belgium, a civilian administration is being put in place in the Netherlands with Austrian-born Reich Commissioner Arthur Seyss-Inquart at the helm. At the time of the German invasion, a total of 140,245 Jews live in the Netherlands: 118,455 with Dutch citizenship, 14,493 from Germany, and 7,297 from other countries, the majority living in Amsterdam.[9] The German administration introduces its first anti-Jewish measures in mid-July. Else and Sigmund terminate their lease and temporarily move in with Richard and Hildegard on *Graaf Florislaan*, remaining with them until the end of the year.[10] Because the Haases are expecting their first child, the couple decides to give the new parents-to-be more space and, starting in December, they rent two rooms in a nearby boarding house on *Jacobus Pennweg*. It is unusually beautiful, they write, with two balconies and a lovely view.

Finally, in January, after months of worry and uneasy silence, the family in the Netherlands receives word from the Rosenfelders in London. During

---

8 Dormitzer, "Experiences."
9 Moore, *Victims and Survivors*, 259.
10 Richard's younger sister, Bettina Olga Haas (1913–1992), lives with them in *Graaf Florislaan* as does his mother, Olga-Haas May (1873–1944), at a later point.

the Battle of Britain, direct communication between the families stopped, but now the Dormitzers and the Haas couple learn at last that their immediate relatives have survived the German air raids and are in good health. To correspond as regularly as possible with each other, the family now frequently uses the more reliable mail service provided by the International Red Cross. On the organization's official forms, with a twenty-five-word maximum, the family conveys messages to each other, often coded to evade potential censorship, ranging from birthday greetings to deportation notices. While family members highly anticipate these short telegram-like messages, delivery is often delayed for weeks.

In the winter of 1941, the Dormitzers look forward to the arrival of their grandson and joyfully welcome Hendrik Paul Herman Haas to the world on February 16. Family letters vividly describe the child's birth, depict the condition of the mother and father and, in general, express pure delight at the occasion. The grandchild is a much-welcome distraction for the family from the ever-changing political situation, which includes the expansion of restrictive measures for Dutch and German Jews. For numerous reasons, Else and Sigmund do not share information about the deteriorating conditions in the Netherlands in their letters to family in London, mentioning neither the compulsory registration of all Jews as of January 10 nor the tumultuous street fights, bloody uprisings, and murders in Amsterdam in February.

The same month, the German administration sets up the Jewish Council, an organizational body tasked with implementing and communicating German measures and directives to the Jewish community. Developing into a multilayered organization over time, the Jewish Council also provides community support for social services, for example, to those in need of accommodations or healthcare. One of its six local branches is in the Westerbork camp, established in October 1939 by the Dutch government in cooperation with the Dutch-Jewish Refugee Committee as a refugee camp for German Jews. The Jewish Council's *Expositur*, headed by Dr. Edwin Sluzker, and the Council's "sole liaison with the German authorities," constitutes an important link to the Central Office for Jewish Emigration created in March 1941.[11] The Central Office, in turn, is responsible for implementing all deportation orders in the Netherlands. Head of the Central Office is SS *Hauptsturmführer* Ferdinand Hugo aus der Fünten.

---

11 Moore, *Victims and Survivors*, 107.

After agreeing at the Wannsee Conference in January 1942 on "mechanizing and optimizing" the extermination of European Jewry, the National Socialists devise measures that quickly escalate the situation in the Netherlands by the summer of the same year.[12] Requiring all Dutch Jews to move to Amsterdam, the German civil administration also orders all German Jews residing in the country to "evacuate" to Westerbork, a refugee camp in the northeast of the country that the National Socialists reorganize as a police transit camp. The euphemism "evacuation" conceals the true intentions motivating these new measures since the deportations to the concentration camps and killing centers in the East begin only a few months later, in July 1942. No one is being "rescued," as the word suggests, on the contrary. At first twice, then once a week, trains leave Westerbork for Auschwitz, Sobibor, Theresienstadt, and Bergen-Belsen.

Richard Haas succeeds in protecting his young family from deportation, as Hildegard explains in a post-war letter to Elisabeth on May 21, 1945:

> Richard, Henkie and myself were summoned to go to Westerbork the same day as Hans (28th January 1942), with great efforts we resulted in getting a respite. It was the very first time anything like that happened here, and it was during the terrible spell of cold (–20 C) that we had to prepare to go. Only the last moment we came to know we could stay. I never really dared to unpack my bags, and until now, I had bags for every one of us lying under the bedstead, the first years for fears of being sent away, the last months in connection with the front coming nearer. Our own situation was never safe at all since Richard had never the good papers and we had to see sent away nearly all our family and many of our friends.[13]

The Dormitzers relocate to Amsterdam in the spring. Until the fall of 1942, they rent a room on *Amstelkade* in Amsterdam-Zuid, then they change their living quarters yet again, taking up space in a boarding house on *Daniel Willinkplein*, today's *Victorieplein*. It is unknown if they receive a deportation notice like their children.[14]

---

12 Ibid., 62.
13 Quote from Hilde Haas's original letter, which is in English, not in German.
14 Bob Moore mentions that some German Jews from Hilversum had to relocate to Amsterdam because Westerbork could no longer accept people as of May 1942. "Even if

During this time, the family letters to Great Britain still do not contain information about the difficulties of everyday life for the aging couple. Lovingly, they write about baby Henk, inquire about their grandchildren and their well-being in London, report on news from family members and friends but are silent about their own fears, daily challenges, or even health concerns. Else and Sigmund are particularly grateful for the family photographs they receive and let their daughter know how much her letters contribute to their well-being, entertainment, and diversion—and to that of other family members and friends who have stayed behind on the European mainland. "The arrival of your beautiful letters is an event for us; you can hardly imagine what happens to such a piece of writing," Else Dormitzer explains on October 15, 1942.

> First, we examine it over and over again, then Richard gets it for Hillo, and they take particular joy in receiving words of praise for Henkie; then the reading takes place at Marie's and Gustav's; and, finally, Aunt Clara receives her share, not even to mention old Retha […].

Throughout the years, the former housekeeper of the Dormitzers from Nuremberg, Retha, has kept in touch, sending holiday presents like knitted socks or gingerbread from Franconia.

Usually, Else's letters close with lines written by her husband, who, as he expresses in August 1942, is worried about his brother Louis and wife Sophie. Not seeking refuge abroad, the family stayed in Nuremberg, and Sigmund now receives notification about their imminent deportation to the Theresienstadt ghetto. Meanwhile, their daughter Lilli—son Max was killed as a soldier during World War I—has gone into hiding in Germany. Sigmund Dormitzer does not hear again from his brother until November 1, and the postcard he receives from Theresienstadt a few months later contains the sad news that his sister-in-law has died. This affects him greatly.

The same month, Marie and Julius Ottenstein, who also escaped to the Netherlands, are deported to Westerbork. After their arrival, the couples

---

the pace of rehousing was determined by shortage of space (Westerbork was deemed full in May, and some German Jews from Hilversum were brought to Amsterdam as a result), the Germans had established most of the bureaucratic institutions they would require to deprive the Jews of their remaining property and effect their deportation." Moore, *Victims and Survivors*, 88–89.

communicate by mail, the Dormitzers helping by sending food packages to the camp. Their son, Dr. Hans Ottenstein (1902–1986), a lawyer, has been in Westerbork since the beginning of the year. In his capacity as head of the Petition Office (*Antragsstelle*), he and his colleagues need to justify to the camp administration "why a prisoner could remain [...], thus, be 'barred' from transport, or why a prisoner would be sent 'on transport.' Different lists allowed inmates to be temporarily held back from deportation."[15] Like the employees of the Jewish Council in Amsterdam, Dutch and German Jews are facing allegations of accommodation and collaboration after May 1945 because of their work with the German occupying forces during the war.[16]

Else Dormitzer's post-war accounts illustrate that, at first, she and her husband succeed at escaping the deportations beginning in July 1942.

> The time of large-scale deportations had begun in Holland. People were taken from their apartments to a collection site and then on to the Westerbork Transit Camp. When we were in danger, they had already planned on picking us up, we spent the day hours at an acquaintance's place. She worked at the Jewish Council and had excellent connections there. One time, when we were in great jeopardy because they had come by to look for us, we even stayed at her place for two weeks. This was possible because this lady had obtained an authorization.[17]

In October, Sigmund has to undergo a medical procedure; one, as Hildegard explains after the war, is scheduled "to buy time" from deportation. He remains in the hospital until the middle of November. His wife pays him daily visits, which means walking over two hours daily, constituting a clear sign of her "strength and vivacity" as she writes jokingly to her daughter in the United Kingdom. After her husband's release in November, he closes one of

---

15 Sandra Ziegler, *Gedächtnis und Identität der KZ-Erfahrung. Niederländische und deutsche Augenzeugenberichte des Holocaust* (Würzburg: Königshausen & Neumann, 2006), 133–134.

16 See, for example, Ido de Haan's essay "The Jewish Honor Court in the Netherlands," in *Jewish Honor Courts. Revenge, Retribution, and Reconciliation in Europe and Israel after the War*, ed. Laura Jokusch and Gabriel N. Finder (Detroit: Wayne State University Press, 2015), 107–136.

17 Dormitzer, "Experiences."

his wife's letters in his usual witty fashion, only thinly concealing, however, the wretchedness of the situation he finds himself in.

> My dear ones! The previous speaker has already anticipated with her usual chattiness (or "write-iness") all I was going to write [...]. Whenever I receive your letters, my yearning to see all of you again grows infinitely. My present company in this house—eight old ladies with a total age of 600 years, my wife the baby among them, me the only man, well, condition of a man—is surely no substitute for you all.

The first months of the new year, 1943, bring no end to the constant restlessness and anxiety the couple is experiencing. The Dormitzers are in close contact with friends and acquaintances in Amsterdam, each day bringing more dreadful news about arrests and deportations. They feel helpless in the face of the deteriorating situation. Still weakened from his operation, Else is also concerned about her husband's slow recovery, and she herself is now dealing with health problems. She cannot sleep and does not have much of an appetite; she is nervous and restless, impatiently waiting for news from loved ones, organizing laundry, mending socks, talking with neighbors in and around the boarding house on *Daniel Willinkplein*. The only family member they manage to see infrequently is Richard, who continues to work in Amsterdam. With daughter Hildegard, they are only in touch through letters or notes passed on by their son-in-law.

Notification for the Dormitzers from the *Expositur* at the Amsterdam Jewish Council to appear in person on Saturday, April 17, 1943 at 11:00 am.

Then, in April, the Dormitzers receive their deportation notice for Theresienstadt, as Else writes in one of her two post-war testimonials.

> In Amsterdam, we received a dispatch at midnight containing a summons to appear before the *SS-Obersturmführer* on the next day at noon (April 17, 1943). There, a speech by him to all invitees: that the German government had arranged, as a special privilege, that an extra transport would be headed to Th. for deserving German and Dutch Jews. There, we could live a truly paradisiacal life, under Jewish self-government, in complete freedom, enjoy the same food rations as the SS, the-ater, movies, and many possibilities for recreation in the sur-rounding area. Those who did not take advantage of this offer could no longer count on respectful treatment (i.e. transport to Poland).[18]

According to a letter from Hildegard to her sister in May 1945, their par-ents were arrested in Amsterdam a month earlier and held captive in the *Hollandsche Schouwburg*, the central collection point for departing transports from the Netherlands. Richard, she writes, succeeds in having his in-laws tem-porarily released from the *Schouwburg,* and the deportation to Theresienstadt in April should ultimately be "considered a favor." Apparently, Richard Haas advocates directly for his parents-in-law with the German administration in The Hague, at the *Referat IV B 4*, in charge of the organization of the mass murder of the Jewish population in the Netherlands. The head of the office is *SS-Sturmbannführer* Wilhelm Zoepf, whom Richard knows from his school days in Munich.[19] He succeeds *"met medewirking van Fräulein Slottke,"*

---

18 Else Dormitzer, "Life in Theresienstadt," Wiener Holocaust Library, P.III.h. (Theresienstadt), no. 560. The file is cited throughout this chapter as "Life." See the appendix for the original document in German and its English translation by Cornelius Partsch. Dormitzer's eyewitness accounts contain different dates about the summons to appear at the Central Office for Emigration in Amsterdam: April 17, 1943, and also April 20. The transport to Theresienstadt departed from Amsterdam on April 21, 1943.

19 NIOD 270d, 1.3, Trial E. Rajakowitsch, Document Haas, 2. After the war, Richard Haas submitted a written statement for the investigation of Erich Rajakovic (spelling also Rajakowitsch). Rajakovic, originally from Austria, was head of the *Referat J* in the Netherlands before it was reorganized and restructured as *Referat IV B4* under Wilhelm Harster's leadership, who, in turn, staffed the new office with Wilhelm Zoepf. Christan Ritz, *Schreibtischtäter vor Gericht. Das Verfahren vor dem Münchener Landgericht wegen der*

the administrative assistant in the office, "who had independent decision-making authority and leverage," to place Else and Sigmund on a transport list to Theresienstadt.[20] "Tell your wife," Richard quotes Gertrud Slottke verbatim, "the parents are old, they are going on a big, long journey and one cannot count on seeing them again."[21]

On Wednesday, April 21, 1943, the first transport to Theresienstadt from the Netherlands is scheduled to leave Amsterdam, "we left, sitting on a comfortable train, four persons per compartment, in possession of our luggage and fifty guilders, which had been given to all travelers. During the journey the SS handed out postcards which we were supposed to write to relatives."[22] On the day of their deportation, the Dormitzers use the Red Cross mail service one last time to contact their children in the United Kingdom. They previously shared that Sigmund's brother Louis was sent to Theresienstadt; now they are encoding their message with reference to him, thereby letting family members know of their own impending deportation: "All healthy. Will meet Louis soon. Had a lovely visit from the Haas family. Henkie adorable. All return their greetings, especially Marie. Always thinking of you, hugs to you and the children, parents."

Deportation der niederländischen Juden (1959–1967) (Paderborn: Ferdinand Schöningh, 2012), 124.

20   Document Haas, 3. See also Elisabeth Kohlhaas, "Gertrud Slottke—Angestellte im niederländischen Judenreferat der Sicherheitspolizei," in *Karrieren der Gewalt. Nationalsozialistische Täterbiographien*, ed. Klaus-Michael Mallmann und Gerhard Paul (Darmstadt: Wissenschaftliche Buchgesellschaft, 2004), 207ff. Starting in the summer of 1943, Gertrud Slottke was responsible for "the complex system of 'provisions,' guaranteeing in the eyes of the National Socialist occupiers a reasonable, orderly procedure of the cleansing of the Netherlands from Jewish people" (ibid., 210).

21   Document Haas, 3.

22   Dormitzer, "Experiences." For the historical background of this transport, including a quote from Else Dormitzer's testimonial account, see Yad Vashem, "Record details (Historical Background)," accessed November 2, 2022. https://deportation.yadvashem.org/index.html?language=en&itemId=5092551.

Sind Alle gesund. Treffen demnächst Louis,
Hatten schönen Besuch aller Haarens,
Henkie reizend. Alle erwidern Grüsse,
besonders Marie. Denken stets Euer,
umarmen Euch und Kinder.

Eltern

21.4.43.

2 JUIN 1943

Red Cross letter from Else and Sigmund to family members on the day of their deportation to Theresienstadt.

**Theresienstädter
Bilder**

Else Dormitzer

Book cover of *Theresienstädter Bilder,* drawing by Otto Treumann.

CHAPTER FOUR

Theresienstadt, 1943–1945

Built by Emperor Joseph II in the second half of the eighteenth century, Terezín is a small fortress town in the Czech Republic approximately thirty-seven miles northwest of Prague. Because of its original purpose as a defense installation and military base, the town reveals a checkerboard layout fortified by ramparts and walls, measuring a mere 700 meters in length and 500 meters in width.[1] Within its star-like, dodecagonal shape, military-style barracks, casemates, and relatively few houses provide accommodations for its estimated 7,168 residents (Census 1930), not even remotely enough for the mass of people interned by the Germans between 1941 and 1945:[2] When the Dormitzers arrive in spring 1943, records list the number of prisoners at 43,806 (June), already a decrease from 50,006 in December 1942.[3] Just outside of Theresienstadt, which is also called the Great Fortress, lies the Small Fortress, a nineteenth-century detention site serving as a transit prison for the Prague Gestapo after 1939.[4]

In November 1941, the SS (*Schutzstaffel*) sets up a Jewish-led administration, charging its prisoners with the implementation of their directives and orders. Shortly after the end of the war, sociologist H. G. Adler, himself interned in Theresienstadt, meticulously details how the complex,

---

1   H. G. Adler, *Theresienstadt 1941–1945. Das Antlitz einer Zwangsgemeinschaft* (Tübingen: Mohr, 1955), 30. The number refers to the internal dimensions of Theresienstadt as listed in Adler; the dodecagonal-like shape measures 1200x920 meters.

2   Ibid., 27. Adler lists a total of 219 houses based on documents from the Jewish Community Prague.

3   Ibid., 689–691. According to Livia Rothkirchen, Theresienstadt held 60,000 prisoners by October 1942. Livia Rothkirchen. *The Jews of Bohemia and Moravia. Facing the Holocaust* (Lincoln: University of Nebraska Press, 2005), 234.

4   Anna Hájková, *The Last Ghetto: An Everyday History of Theresienstadt* (Oxford: Oxford University Press, 2020), 7.

all-encompassing administrative body worked and developed and which challenges it continuously faced until the end of the war.[5] Throughout its four-year history, the national composition of prisoners, along with the ghetto's manifold functions, undergo constant transformation, complicating, as Michael Berenbaum notes, straight-forward classification of Theresienstadt within the camp and ghetto system in the post-war years: "Historians are not quite sure how to describe it; thus, in accounts and memoirs four different terms are used to refer to its diverse functions: garrison city, ghetto, concentration camp, and transit camp."[6] He continues:

> It was the anteroom to Auschwitz for Jews from Bohemia and Moravia and for "prominents"—men and women of influence, the elderly and those who served in World War I. And it was positioned by the Nazis as a model ghetto, a place that demonstrated the Führer's "decency" to the Jews. In reality, it was a means of concealing the Reich's actual intentions from an inquiring world. This duality, along with the feverish cultural life, organized by those interned there, gave the ghetto an almost surrealistic quality.[7]

The *SS* sends more than 143,000 women, children, and men from across Europe to Terezín. "Among them were 74,000 Jews from the Protectorate of Bohemia and Moravia," writes historian Anna Hájková, "600 from the Sudeten area, 1,400 Slovaks, 42,000 German and 15,000 Austrian Jews,

---

5   H. G. Adler (1910–1988) survived the Shoah in different camps after his initial transport from Theresienstadt to Auschwitz. He emigrated to the United Kingdom in 1947, where he lived until his death. Several publications on Adler have appeared in recent years in English see, for instance: Julia Creet, Sara Horowitz, and Amira Bojadzija-Dan, eds., *H. G. Adler: Life, Literature, Legacy* (Evanston: Northwestern University Press, 2016); and Lynn Wolff, ed., *A Modernist in Exile. The International Reception of H. G. Adler (1910–1988)* (Oxford: Legenda, 2019).

6   Michael Berenbaum, "Foreword," in *In Memory's Kitchen: A Legacy from the Women of Theresienstadt,* ed. Cara de Silva, transl. Bianca Steiner Brown (Northvale: J. Aronson, 1996), ix. See also Peter Klein, "Theresienstadt: Ghetto oder Konzentrationslager?," in *Theresienstädter Studien und Dokumente,* ed. Jaroslava Milotová et al. (Prague: Sefer, 2005), 28–35. A more recent discussion can be found in the introduction by Anna Hájková to *The Last Ghetto.*

7   Michael Berenbaum, *A Promise to Remember. The Holocaust in the Words and Voices of its Survivors* (Boston: Bulfinch Press, 2003), 10.

4,900 from the Netherlands, 466 from Denmark, and 1,150 from Hungary." Thirty-four thousand people die in the camp between 1941 and 1945.[8]

In the afternoon of April 22, 1943, Transport XXIV/1 from Amsterdam reaches the town of *Bohušovice*, a short distance from the Theresienstadt ghetto.[9] Greeting the deportees upon arrival are shouting, orders, and "lots of *SS* to welcome us."[10] The Dormitzers need to complete the last two and a half kilometers to the ghetto on foot, carrying their belongings as best as they can in their hands and on their backs. Totally exhausted, "more dead than alive," after being shoved with more than 300 people down a dusty country road, they arrive in Theresienstadt and are separated upon arrival, uneasily waiting for the things to come over the course of the evening: luggage inspection and removal of all "food, medications, toiletry, writing tools, all powered items," including the fifty Dutch guilders previously approved in the Netherlands. It does not take long for the couple to realize that what they had hoped to be true about Theresienstadt—a life "in complete freedom," enjoying "the same food rations as the *SS*, theater, movies, and many possibilities for recreation in the surrounding area," as *SS Hauptsturmführer* aus der Fünten had tried to make them believe in Amsterdam just a few days earlier—is not. Far from it. For hours on end, the couple is standing on their feet, aching, tired, waiting

---

8   Hájková, *The Last Ghetto*, 7.
9   In Else Dormitzer's accounts as well as in other primary and secondary sources on the Theresienstadt ghetto, *Bohušovice* is also referred to by its German name, *Bauschowitz*. No train tracks extend into Theresienstadt in April 1943, and all incoming and outgoing transports are cleared outside the confines of the former military town until the transportation line is completed in June later that year. Adler, *Theresienstadt 1941–1945*, 262. For more information on this transport, see Record Details, Yad Vashem, accessed November 2, 2022, https://deportation.yadvashem.org/index.html?language=en&itemId=5092551: "The first transport to Theresienstadt departed on April 21, 1943. According to the plan, the transport should have set out in early March, but, due to epidemic typhus and overcrowding, the gates of the ghetto had been shut forcing Eichmann to postpone the departure. To avoid the languid pace of a special deportation train which usually involved several days in transit, the railroad administration in Utrecht proposed that the Jews be sent in passenger cars coupled to a regular train that would proceed at ordinary speed. Reichskommissar of the Netherlands, Arthur Seyss-Inquart, was also interested in depicting the deportation from the Netherlands to Theresienstadt as a 'relocation of residence' (Wohnsitzverlegung), deriving utility from this propaganda. Therefore, he proposed that the train depart directly from Amsterdam and not from the Westerbork transit camp. Eichmann had no objection to this."
10 Unless otherwise noted, quotes in the main text of this chapter are directly from Dormitzer's eyewitness accounts and her poetry collection, which were translated by Cornelius Partsch. All other translations, including secondary materials, are mine.

to be registered, all without water or food. They need to undress in front of strangers so that their clothes and bodies can be searched for impermissible items; in the meantime, an "SS officer yells that he would give the order to shoot if anyone made a sound. [...] All accompanied by shouting and beatings of those who still had money or jewelry on them; they were taken to prison." Nevertheless, Else succeeds in hiding her diary from the watchful eyes of the guards, eventually smuggling it inside.

The couple spends the night in the "sluice," as the inspection site for all incoming and departing transports is called, hardly finding sleep on the few dirty mattresses on the floor in the turmoil around them. After their work category is determined the next morning—Sigmund and Else are exempt from work because of their age—they receive their food cards and are allocated their new quarters. At least, they are housed in the same building (L 116/*Seestraße*) but separated by gender "each with sixteen others in a small room." "Not the expected and promised senior residences," she writes after the war, "for which our compatriots from Germany had been robbed of all their money, but rather overcrowded rooms, devoid of any kind of comfort, mostly in barracks or housing blocks." No bed, table, chair, or dresser; only a bag of hay as a substitute bed. Until her liberation in the spring of 1945, Else moves a total of seventeen times within the ghetto.

The shock created by the arrival in the camp, the so-called "admission shock," as she aptly terms the experience, "which felt like we were totally paralyzed," strikes them without mercy. Utterly unprepared for the harsh reality of Theresienstadt, the couple is suddenly confronted with hunger, dirt, stench, vermin, overcrowded living quarters, and masses of people. Understanding the need to adjust quickly to the new conditions, Else starts pulling herself out of her numbness after a few days "since I recognized that there was no other way to persevere in the camp." She tries to find better accommodations and food provisions for her and her husband but to no avail. However, she succeeds in organizing a mattress for Sigmund, whose physical health and emotional wellbeing are further weakened after their arrival.

Before their deportation to Theresienstadt a few days earlier, Sigmund had hoped to see his older brother Louis again, but, instead of the anticipated reunion in the ghetto, he learns of his brother's death and is grief-stricken. His health declines rapidly over the next several months, accelerated by the insufficient nutrition Sigmund receives as a non-worker with the lowest calorie allocation. Else devotes her time to taking care of her husband, leaving no stone unturned in trying to improve his deteriorating condition. In October

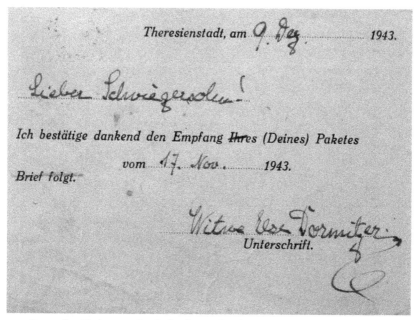

Postcard to Else's son-in-law Richard Haas dated on the day of Sigmund's death, the
signature reads "Widow Else Dormitzer."

1943, a doctor requests additional food rations for him, but by the middle
of November, the seventy-four-year-old is admitted to the hospital, where
he is diagnosed with famine edema, a common disease in Theresienstadt
caused by malnutrition. Despite the tending love he receives from his wife,
including her food rations, and the tireless care by doctors and nurses in
Theresienstadt, Sigmund Dormitzer dies on December 9, 1943. His wife is
devastated. To inform her children in Hilversum and London of their father's
death, she signs and mails the camp's official parcel confirmation form back
to Richard Haas, thereby acknowledging receipt of their last care package.
This pre-printed notification in the form of a postcard cannot include any
personal information, and, instead of signing it with both her first and last
name, she simply lists her name as "Widow Else Dormitzer." It takes several
months for the card to reach Hilversum and, after that, for the news to reach
the United Kingdom. Finally, in January 1944, Else is allowed to write a post-
card to her loved ones, providing more details about her husband's death
and concluding her lines with a bleak assessment of the current situation:
"My life is empty and dreary, only work is holding me up, I gave seventy-
five talks and have more planned for the coming weeks." Sporadically, she

receives news from her children, constantly worrying about their wellbeing. Whenever their care packages reach her in Theresienstadt, she records the delivery dates and contents in her diary. From Sweden too, one of five neutral European countries during World War II, she receives these highly welcomed food parcels; a family friend, Claire Nielsen, is putting them together for her and sending them to the German-occupied Protectorate along with news about her children in the Netherlands and in Great Britain with whom she is in touch.

Today, Theresienstadt is perhaps best remembered for its enduring artistic legacy, ranging from the children's drawings and poetry on display at the Jewish Museum in Prague to original musical performances such as Viktor Ullmann's opera *The Emperor of Atlantis,* its German-language libretto written by Peter Kien.[11] And indeed, many prisoners in Theresienstadt found artistic outlets to express the traumatic experience of deportation and imprisonment in multiple languages and forms. Some created art to bear witness or to document daily life, yet for others, as Sybil H. Milton and Marjorie Lamberti have shown in their work, it served as a temporary flight from reality or as a strategy for survival. Diaries and testimonies from Theresienstadt convey the significance of art created in extremis, often providing additional information on the organization and reception of the ghetto's manifold cultural activities. However, precisely because of its prominent cultural afterlife, historian Sybil Milton cautions us in viewing Theresienstadt as an anomaly in the German camp system. This, she writes, creates a dangerous myth, sidetracking us from the perpetrators' real intentions within the context of the Final Solution. Deceiving the world, as she writes in her essay "Art in the Context of Theresienstadt," was part of the make-believe machinery of the Nazis.

> The Theresienstadt ghetto was thus, as we now know, a camp designed as a link in the chain that inevitably led to the gas chambers and also an elaborate hoax to deceive international opinion. As part of this depiction, the SS tolerated

---

11 Margot Heukäufer's book on Peter Kien contains invaluable information on Kien's life, work, and art, including his original Theresienstadt poetry and one-acts plays *Der Böse Traum* (1943) and *An der Grenze* (1943). See Margot Heukäufer, *Und es gibt so wenig Menschen: Das kurze Leben des Künstlers Peter Kien* (Prague: Helena Osvaldová, 2009).

some cultural activities, including theater, music, lectures, and concerts. Other cultural activities, such as art and teaching the children were not specifically prohibited, but carried risks if discovered. But while we know that Terezín was nothing but a way-station to the killing centers, the posthumous fame of Theresienstadt is based primarily on the myth created by this hoax.[12]

Shortly after the ghetto starts operating in late 1941, prisoners form the so-called Office for Leisure-Time Activities (*Freizeitgestaltung*) to jumpstart the organization of cultural activities, creating a variety of highly successful programs, including, for example, musical and theater performances of new and original works. [13]

> Kicking off the Office for Leisure-Time Activities triggered a true chain reaction. Choir rehearsals started in barracks, voice lessons, singing lessons, language courses, theater performances; chess groups formed, sporting events were organized, the first public lectures took place, evenings of music and entertainment with recitations, songs, accordion music, followed later by chamber music matinees, orchestra concerts, opera performances, at first concertante, cabaret evenings, coffee house soirees, all of this in a variety and over-

---

12 Sybil Milton, "Art in the Context of Theresienstadt," in *Art, Music, Education as Strategies for Survival: Theresienstadt*, ed. Anne Dutlinger (New York: Herodias, 2000), 18.

13 A number of excellent articles and books on musical and theatrical performances in and from Theresienstadt include Michael Beckerman, "Postcard from New York-Trio from Terezín," *Music & Politics* 1, no. 1 (2007): 1–19; Ulrike Migdal, ed., *Und die Musik spielt dazu. Chansons und Satiren aus Theresienstadt* (Munich: Piper, 1986); Lisa Peschel, ed., *Performing Captivity, Performing Escape: Cabarets and Plays from the Terezín/Theresienstadt Ghetto* (London: Seagull Books, 2014); eadem, "Das Theater in Theresienstadt und das Zweite Tschechische Kabarett: 'Geistiger Widerstand'?," in *Theresienstädter Studien und Dokumente*, ed. Jaroslava Milotová and Anna Hájková (Prague: Sefer, 2008), 84–114; Rebecca Rovit and Alvin Goldfarb, eds., *Theatrical Performances during the Holocaust: Text, Documents, Memoirs* (Baltimore: Johns Hopkins University Press, 1999); Amy Lynn Wlodarski, "Musical Memories of Terezín in Transnational Perspective," in *Dislocated Memories: Jews, Music, and Postwar German Culture*, ed. Tina Frühoff and Lily Hirsch (Oxford: Oxford University Press, 2014), 57–74; and eadem, "Musical Testimonies of Terezín and the Possibilities of Contrapuntal Listening," *Music & Politics* 16, no. 2 (2022): 1–21.

abundance that is hard to believe given the large numbers of prisoners. The arts inexorably conquered their territory: the barracks, the blocks, the courtyards.[14]

Not surprisingly, after years of steady engagement in public and community life, Else Dormitzer readily lends her services to the Office for Leisure-Time Activities, an organization she describes as a "bright spot" in the dismal day-to-day of Theresienstadt. Starting in the summer of 1943, she regularly delivers public presentations, visiting different buildings, including the nursing home and the makeshift hospital space in the "Genie Barracks."

> I was among the few who did not shy away from speaking in all sections of the tuberculosis ward, and patients appreciated this greatly. They reached into their bread bags and cut off a slice for me. I accepted these gladly, the hunger was stronger than any sense of caution or fear I felt of contracting the disease.

The philosopher and university professor Emil Utitz, head of the Central Library in Theresienstadt and organizer of several lecture series, writes about the popularity and success of the presentations he organizes:

> One such speaker series on significant thinkers of the past attracted 600-800 people. Although these presentations took place in late fall, in the huge, unheated attic of the barracks while the ice-cold wind howled through the skylights; and people had to climb up unlit staircases, heading home in complete darkness. We were able to verify these positive impressions, for one, not only through conversations after the presentations but also by receiving book requests from our clients. One can clearly assert that everyone who had something to say and could do so well soon had a large audience, one following them affectionally and loyally.[15]

---

14 Migdal, *Und die Musik spielt dazu. Chansons und Satiren aus Theresienstadt*, 15–16.
15 Reinhard Mehring, ed., *Ethik nach Theresienstadt. Späte Texte des Prager Philosophen Emil Utitz* (Würzburg: Königshausen & Neumann, 2015), 74.

For her own presentations, Else Dormitzer revisits earlier topics of interest and expertise. Her first public lecture in August 1943, for example, is entitled "Famous Jewish Women," drawing on her previous publication with the Central Union of German Citizens of Jewish Faith in 1925. However, she also creates new presentations, among them travel reports ("Travel to Scandinavia"), impressions from her time in the Netherlands ("Life in Holland"), or recollections of her work as a writer ("From the Diary of a Journalist"). Additionally, she entertains her audience with personal stories and anecdotes from pre-war life in Nuremberg that she bases on entries from the family's guest books ("From My Guest Books"). She tremendously enjoys creating a space of respite for fellow inmates, allowing them to escape "for an hour from the atmosphere of Theresienstadt" to evoke memories of a better time. In her two years in the camp, she gives a total of two-hundred and seventy-five talks, noting the title, date, and location of each in her diary and, when running out of space, on single sheets of paper.[16]

From April to June 1944, Else needs to take a forced break from her social and cultural engagements. An infection caused by vermin sees her being admitted to the so-called "Septical Barracks," a makeshift wooden structure serving as the hospital's surgical department. Else undergoes several operations and prolonged treatment, spending ten weeks in total in the medical unit with twenty people to the room and no bandaging materials. "Doctors and nurses were brave. Almost all caregivers were deported to Auschwitz in October 1944," writes Dr. Hermann Strauß, himself a doctor in Theresienstadt.[17] Only a few months after the death of her husband, as she writes after the war, her will to live is almost non-existent, feeling "an abysmal indifference towards everything." Her sister Marie, now also a widow, arrives in Theresienstadt from Westerbork in the spring of 1944 and successfully pulls her out of her lethargy and depressive episodes.

When Else is finally discharged from the hospital in June 1944, she shows her appreciation for the care received by gifting the head physician an original poem. As requested, she initially finds housing in the "Genie

16 See also Adler, *Theresienstadt*, 598.
17 Harro Jenss und Peter Reinicke, eds., *Der Arzt Hermann Strauß 1868–1944. Autobiographische Notizen und Aufzeichnungen aus dem Ghetto Theresienstadt* (Berlin: Hentrich & Hentrich, 2014). See also Adler's *Theresienstadt* (chapter 16) and Hájková's *The Last Ghetto* (chapter 4) for further discussion of medical care in the ghetto.

Barracks" but soon needs to move to the "Dutch Barracks," most likely because of her affiliation with the Dutch transports and her labor status. While her age officially exempts her from work, she is constantly seeking and taking on different jobs—such as peeling potatoes and pushing carts of coal—to receive additional food rations that help in saving herself and her sister from starvation.[18] After the SS orders mass deportations to the killing centers in the East in the fall of 1944 to greatly reduce the number of prisoners in Theresienstadt, Else finds a new position with the post office, a job she holds until the camp's liberation in May 1945.[19] In her eyewitness account, she details her responsibilities, writing that her many tasks include compiling an extensive card index "of all deportees and all those who were assigned to work outside of the ghetto" before being directed at the end of the war "by order of the SS" to destroy the record, "so that it should never be known how many thousands of inmates were actually at Theresienstadt."

Poetry in Theresienstadt

Apart from journaling everyday life and actively participating in cultural events in the ghetto, Else Dormitzer also writes poetry, first sharing her poetic texts publicly with an audience on February 29, 1944. While it is

---

18 See also Adler, *Theresienstadt*, 597–598.

19 Else Dormitzer sheds some light on her work for the post office in her two Theresienstadt-specific accounts. An interviewer, who remains unnamed, also mentions the position in another document, part of a collection of post-war reports for the *Rijksinstituut Voor Oorlogsdocumentatie*. Written in Dutch, the eight-page summary from 1950 contains additional information about life in Theresienstadt, which is not included in the eyewitness accounts, for example, on Sigmund Dormitzer's funeral. The difference between files in the Wiener Holocaust Library in London and the NIOD in Amsterdam is that the latter is not a first-person account but a third-person summary of a conversation with Else Dormitzer in which bias on the part of the interviewer is apparent (see, for example, the introductory comments labeled as *opmerkingen*). This, in turn, is informed by the post-war context in the Netherlands surrounding German-Jewish collaboration and cooperation with the Nazis (also see endnote 16, chapter 3) as well as Dormitzer's age, gender, and social status. The NIOD document forms the basis for Anna Hajková's assessment of Else Dormitzer in *The Last Ghetto*, 121, even though Hajková's endnotes mistakenly attribute its source to the Wiener Holocaust Library file and mislabel the file number. The same holds true for a later comment (ibid., 81); here, Hajková cites the NIOD file when she means to quote the Wiener Holocaust Library file since the NIOD file does not contain that information. *Nederlands Instituut voor Oorlogsdocumentatie* (NOID), 250d, 501. It is mentioned in this document that Else intervened in Theresienstadt to save her sister Marie from deportation (p. IV).

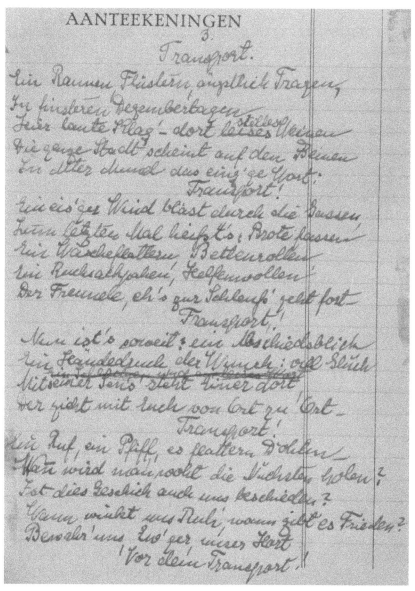

Else Dormitzer's original poem "Transport" in her diary from Theresienstadt.

unknown how many people are present in L 116 for her reading from the "Theresienstadt Cycle"—as she calls the collection in her diary—she is certainly not alone in wanting to express the experience of persecution, deportation, and imprisonment through poetry. It is an activity shared by many other prisoners in the camp and ghetto system, with poetry taking

on particular importance in the cultural life of the Theresienstadt ghetto.[20] More than four hundred German-language poems alone have been preserved in archives, anthologies, and single publications. Prisoners turn to express their experience through formal structures, traditional language patterns, and rhyme schemes, their texts displaying the influence of different lyrical traditions, personal preferences, and artistic abilities. The poems' heterogeneity, their diversity in content, language, and form, is one of the distinguishing marks of German-language poetry from Theresienstadt. While fulfilling different functions at different times, writing poetry, at its most basic, reminds its creators of their agency as "thinking, autonomous human beings" in the concentrationary universe.[21]

Judging by conventional literary standards, fellow inmate H. G. Adler is not particularly impressed by the quality of poems produced, describing the prisoners' fervor in creating poetry a *Theresienstädter Reimkrankheit*, a "rhyming disease," that, apparently, also afflicted him. Philipp Manes, a central figure in the "Orientation Office" (*Orientierungsdienst*), is also critical of the quality of poems produced; overall, however, he reacts more positively to this phenomenon, recognizing instead the testimonial value of many poems as well as their ability to provide comfort to prisoners and to construct a bond when openly recited. Therefore, Manes decides to elicit and collect texts, organize poetry recitals, and set up at least two poetry competitions. Taking place in 1942 and 1944 respectively, they each receive more than 200 entries "written on all kinds of paper, including—please believe me—on toilet paper."[22]

> Some people brought me verses that they had written here. I found some so remarkable that I said to myself that there must be a way to preserve them, so that these good poems could later be made available to the public to promote young

---

20 See the bibliography for my publications on German-language poetry written during the Shoah.

21 Sara Horowitz, *Voicing the Void: Muteness and Memory in Holocaust Fiction* (Albany: SUNY Press, 1997), 59.

22 Philipp Manes, *As If It Were Life. A WWII Diary From The Theresienstadt Ghetto*, ed. Ben Barkow and Klaus Leist, trans. Janet Forster, Klaus Leist, and Ben Barkow (New York: Palgrave Macmillan, 2009), 59. Originally from Berlin, Philipp Manes owned a fur store before the war. His diary from Theresienstadt contains invaluable information on the cultural activities in Theresienstadt, including the poetry competitions he arranged. When the SS sent more than 18,000 to the killing centers in Eastern Europe in October 1944, he and his wife Gertrud were put on the last transport to Auschwitz on October 28, 1944.

talent and encourage creativity. I initiated a competition—deadline: December 20 [1942]—and put an announcement in a circular and also posted one on the notice board. It was a great success.[23]

Joined in 1942 by Fritz Janowitz, head (*Gebäudeältester*) of the "Magdeburg Barracks," Manes, along with the head of the Central Library, Emil Utitz, evaluates the submissions.

In 1944, the jury invites the winners to a public evening recital, handing out books and food as prizes for award recipients.[24] However, the day of the event, August 3, creates logistical challenges for Manes, apparently leading to the removal of select texts from the reading. "My freedom was taken away because the censors interfered and declared a number of the poems unsuitable."[25] In her autobiography, *Three Years in Theresienstadt*, the poet Gerty Spies (1897–1997) recalls this special evening:

> During the summer of 1944, Manes organized a contest for poets, and without my knowing it, he entered the poems I had left with him. I found out that I was one of the winners. An evening was chosen when all the winners would read their own poems. Long before the set time the attic was filled with listeners. [...] We could observe a tension in our audience, just as before a major event; the searing heat of the day, which still filled the room in these evening hours and made breathing difficult, could not chase away our guests. At last our friend Manes climbed onto the wooden throne. He welcomed with a few words those who had come to give and those who had come to take. He went on briefly about this plan to "my poets," as he so kindly and sincerely called us, recite one after the other, and then finally he distributed the slips of paper to the audience on which were to note what and whom they had

---

23 Ibid.
24 Ibid. The jury's selection criteria are unknown. In 1942, Manes makes a preliminary selection, passing on approximately forty poems to Utiz and Janowitz. "I made the first selection, separating the wheat from the chaff. A lot were unusable, doggerel suitable [only] for club and family meetings, the intentions generally better than the results. Thematically, they were rather one-sided: food, rations, housing shortages."
25 Manes, *As If It Were Life*, 222.

liked best. It was to be a referendum as to whose voices could warm the listeners' hearts best.[26]

Spies's recollections are compelling in that they describe an event in which poems are publicly presented that passed internal censorship, highlighting the need for prior intervention because of a perceived danger emanating from critical texts. Fearful of possible repercussions should her poems be discovered, Spies decides early on to never leave them unattended and to always carry them with her.

> In those days it began to be dangerous to write. The inspections, the searching of our houses increased. Several painters whose pictures of Theresienstadt were found during a search by the SS—due to the carelessness of a prisoner—had to pay for their courage with their lives. What to do? My roommates advised me, my friend Herta implored me, to bury or even to burn the written evidence of my camp experience. I could not bring myself to do it. To bury—that would mean to let it decay, and to burn it—that I really could not do. To leave the pages unwatched in the room during the hours of works meant to put the others in danger. No hiding place was safe. And so it happened that I went to work every day with a heavy travel bag over my shoulders, and at night I switched between different hiding places—between the wall and plank, at the bottom of a knapsack, in a sack of straw—and in the morning I recovered them and took them with me. This I did every day, until the day of liberation. And luck was with me.[27]

Writing utensils such as pen, pencil, and paper are often difficult to find. Gerty Spies, for example, writes her poems on packing paper she secretly takes from the mica workshop, and Else Dormitzer includes them in her diary from 1943 or on additional scraps of paper.[28] With the scarcity of basic

---

26   Gerty Spies, *My Years in Theresienstadt. How One Woman Survived the Holocaust*, trans. Jutta R. Tragnitz (Amherst, NY: Prometheus Books, 1997), 104–105.
27   Spies, *My Years in Theresienstadt*, 96.
28   Ibid., 67. On page 62ff, we find a detailed description of the mica workshop: "It was a workshop within a large barrack, where mica-schist was split very fine, until it was like paper and flexible. We sat in groups of twelve at long tables, bent over the work all day

writing supplies, memory comes to play a prominent role in the creation of the poem, often functioning not only as a substitute for pen and paper but also as a secure, mobile storage unit. This way, poems are accessible and safely retrievable everywhere and at any time. "My poetic creations often were long and therefore difficult to retain in memory," writes Spies.

> Then I started the habit (today I cannot fathom how in my physical weakness I summoned the tenacity) with unrelenting energy, while forming and shaping word for word and line for line, to chisel them into my memory, always repeating them again anew in my mind, going on a little, and then repeating all of it again, and so forth. And all that without letting slip away my underlying mood necessary for creating. I held on to them, they held on me—together we held each other, my creatures and I.[29]

Literary scholar and writer Ruth Klüger (1931–2020), who is ten years old when she arrives from Vienna with her mother in 1942, goes a step further, explicitly highlighting the therapeutic dimensions of creating poetry in her award-winning post-war autobiography *weiter leben. Eine Jugend*.[30] Writing poetry, she illustrates, be it in the mind or on paper, keeps her from emotional disintegration, preserving her sanity. The creative act of finding and establishing one's voice constitutes both a poetic and therapeutic act. Giving language to trauma, that is, attempting to put the experienced into words and to arrange linguistic fragments into a unified, meaningful whole, is of primary importance to her. In its regularly structured and often conventional form, the poem emerges as a compact, stable unit of language, serving as a counterweight to the chaotic and unpredictable world around her.

> They are children's poems, wanting to counter the chaos of the everyday through their regularity, a poetic and therapeutic attempt to stem the tide of this senseless and destructive

---

long, and gave it all the strength we had. The summer was unbelievably hot, the barrack hot and sweltering. The women talked about home."

29 Ibid., 72–73.

30 Ruth Klüger, *weiter leben. Eine Jugend* (Munich: dtv, 1994). The English version of Klüger's autobiography appeared in the United States in 2003 as *Still Alive: A Holocaust Girlhood Remembered*. See bibliography for full citation.

circus in which we were drowning with a linguistic wholeness; basically, the oldest aesthetic goal. The person who only lives through the event without rhymes or thoughts is in danger of losing their mind; I did not lose my mind, I made rhymes.[31]

Searching for adequate expressions and, ultimately, for one's own voice come to the fore in creating poetic texts, at once validating and liberating the self emotionally. "The nights did not let me sleep," Gerty Spies writes in *Three Years in Theresienstadt*.

> [...] and while the regular breathing of my companions filled the cramped room with a muffled heaviness, I lay awake, tossing back and forth, forming images with feverish delight and anguish until the images which invaded me had been transformed into language. Only with the early morning prayer of the blackbird did I fall into liberating sleep, often crying with gratitude. I had done my work.[32]

While Klüger and Spies emphasize the usefulness and even practicality of poetry within Theresienstadt, stressing its potential to create stability in a world turned upside down, literary scholars like Frieda W. Aaron, Alan Mintz, and David Roskies situate the choice for poetry within a particular tradition of Jewish writing: namely, as a reaction to persecution and destruction. James E. Young reminds us that, as the Torah and Talmud teach, once evil is witnessed, it needs to be described and reported so that it can be remembered.

> As a traditional definition of witness, this obligation becomes significant in both of its parts: not only is a witness described as someone who both knows and sees an event, but, as elaborated in Talmud (Sanhedrin 30a), once an unjust event is known, in must by law be reported. And if one can become a witness merely be knowing of an event, then implicit in the testimonial act seems to be the possibility for making more witnesses by informing others of events.[33]

---

31 Klüger, *weiter leben*, 126–127.
32 Spies, *My Years in Theresienstadt*, 72.
33 James E. Young, *Writing and Rewriting the Holocaust: Narrative and the Consequences of Interpretation* (Bloomington: Indiana University Press, 1988), 18.

In her book on women's poetry from the Ravensbrück concentration camp, literary scholar Constanze Jaiser argues that this testimonial dimension of poetry is, in fact, its distinguishing characteristic and the appropriate lens for approaching these texts critically.[34] Consequently, the imperative of writing also serves as the imperative for future remembrance. Just as the camp and ghetto diarists want to bear witness to the events unfolding around them and to create durable documents of the terror they experience, so do many poets, she argues. Chaim Kaplan also notes this dimension in his diary from Warsaw: "It is difficult to write, but I consider it an obligation and am determined to fulfill it with my last ounce of energy. I will write a scroll of agony in order to remember the past in the future."[35] Stephen Spender expands this frame even further by stressing the importance of didactics in the Jewish tradition of writing poetry. The writers, he argues, do not only write for themselves but as a voice for their people required to fulfill the task of future remembrance and teaching about the event. "His purposes are didactic and mystical, not aesthetic."[36]

Spies and Klüger illustrate that it is not only the final product, the poem itself, that is of significance but also the process and motivation leading to its creation. In trying to understand and translate the new conditions and their imminent consequences, many prisoners resort not only to a condensed form but also to a language known and familiar to them. Characterized by the immediacy of the Holocaust, the poems emerge in an interplay of different temporal layers—in demarcation to the past, as an immediate reaction to the present, and in anticipation of an unknown future. That, which in post-war discourse is often deemed "unspeakable," is thus rendered "speakable" while the Holocaust unfolds. Writing poetry becomes a way to make sense of the world and to preserve the self in the face of physical and mental dissolution, despite the fallibility of language and its potential flaws of representation. "There were two ways in which to confront the unbearable reality," poet Rose Ausländer observes:

---

34 Constanze Jaiser, *Poetische Zeugnisse: Gedichte aus dem Frauen-Konzentrationslager Ravensbrück, 1939–1945* (Stuttgart: Metzler, 2000).

35 Chaim Kaplan, *Scroll of Agony. The Warsaw Diary of Chaim A. Kaplan*, trans. Abraham I. Katsh (New York: Macmillan, 1965), 34.

36 Stephen Spender, "Introduction," in Abba Kovner and Nelly Sachs, *Selected Poems*, trans. Shirley Kaufman and Nurit Orchan (Harmondsworth: Penguin, 1971), 8–9.

either one succumbed to desperation, or one lived in a differ-
ent reality, a spiritual one. We Jews, who were condemned to
die, needed to be consoled unutterably. And while we waited
for death, some of us lived in dream words—our traumatic
home in homelessness. Writing was life. Survival.[37]

Additionally, actively remembering and reciting one's own compositions
and those of others also fulfill essential functions—the success of the poetry
competitions Manes organizes may serve as one example. Prisoners in
Theresienstadt value the opportunity to perform their work before an audi-
ence, while the organizers can count on appreciative and attentive listeners.
Such public gatherings, for example, have the ability to create a communal
space in which individual experience, as expressed in the poem, manifests
itself collectively, generating a temporary moment of identification for the
audience. It is Ruth Klüger who stresses poetry's ability to console during
uncertain times, helping to "magically" dissolve time. For prisoners, she
writes, the active recall of stable, often rhyming, linguistic structures was par-
ticularly important:

> Many inmates found comfort in the poems they had memo-
> rized earlier in life. Naturally, one can ask why reciting poetry
> in this particular setting is so comforting. [...] It seems to
> me that the content of these lines was only of secondary
> importance and that the verse form itself, the stable language,
> helped us. Or perhaps even this is too much of an interpre-
> tation, and one should state first and foremost that poems
> structure time and are literally a pastime activity. When times
> are bad one can do nothing better than to chase them away,
> and each poem becomes a magic charm.[38]

During the endless hours of roll call in Auschwitz, where she and her mother
are subsequently deported, Klüger focuses on recalling single words and
lines from one of Germany's best-known classical writers, Friedrich Schiller

---

37 Rose Ausländer, "Alles kann Motiv sein," in eadem, *Gesammelte Werke*, vol. 3: *Hügel,
aus Äther, unwiderruflich. Gedichte und Prosa 1966–1975*, ed. Helmut Braun (Frankfurt:
S. Fischer, 1984), 286.
38 Klüger, *weiter leben*, 123–124.

(1759–1805). She uses them over and over again to divert her attention and to avoid collapsing from physical exhaustion. The process of recitation is automated, she writes, as if consciously "playing a record in her head," but it aids in passing dreadful times and, ultimately, in surviving the exertion.

> Schiller's ballads became my roll-call poems. With them, I could stand in the sun for hours on end without collapsing because there was always a next line to recite. And whenever I could not remember the following line, I could think about it extensively before thinking of my own weakness. Then, possibly, roll call was over, and I could turn off the record in my head around the part: "Only eternal and serious things / Be her metallic mouth's devotion." One could toddle off and drink water. Until the next roll call.[39]

Else Dormitzer's Poetry Collection *Theresienstädter Bilder*

In line with Spies's and Klüger's observations and most other German-language poems from Theresienstadt, Dormitzer's poetic renditions are neither encrypted nor experimental but conventionally structured units with simple rhyme schemes in which everyday life is captured, processed, and represented. This simple yet descriptive form of expression is a continuation of her early creative work, in particular of the numerous children's verses of the 1920s, grounding her own response to trauma within familiar and traditional parameters. Thus, her "pictures" (*Bilder*) constitute poetic snapshots of individual moments aimed at making the experience of loss, deportation, and internment visible and accessible.

The book's original cover from 1945 shows a drawing of a small picturesque town surrounded by hills and barbed wire, the latter directly offsetting the idyllic impression created by the visual representation.[40] A short preface opens the collection, in which Dormitzer reveals a performative dimension

---

39 Ibid., 124.
40 Otto Treumann (1919–2001), a well-known graphic artist, created the illustration for the cover. He is also related to the Dormitzers, and the couples' guest books contain at least one of his drawings.

of her poetry by informing the reader that the texts included in this volume were publicly recited in Theresienstadt and that its publication is the result of a promise she made in captivity. From the beginning, she establishes herself as a direct, credible, and reliable witness of the Holocaust. Simultaneously, she discloses other witnesses, who attest to her having been in Theresienstadt, to her having written these poems, and for these poems to have been communally recited. Thus, poems and publication serve as printed proof of the actuality of writer and events, a defining characteristic of the literature of testimony.[41]

The preface is framed as a dedication to her former fellow inmates, her "companions in suffering," which is illustrated by repetition in both the opening and closing sentences. "To you, who were my companions in suffering in Theresienstadt, this small book is dedicated. [...] It is in the spirit of this bond that I dedicate 'Pictures of Theresienstadt' to you." She speaks to her readers directly, and the use of the second person plural pronoun *euch* (you) in the German original expresses not only plurality but also a strong familiarity with this group. A few lines later, she defines this familiarity further by alluding to a strong, irrevocable bond because of the shared lived experience of their Theresienstadt past. This bond, she states, is thicker than blood. The verb choice in the opening and closing lines of the German original is noteworthy since *widmen* (first sentence) and *weihen* (final sentence) denote two slightly different meanings even though they can indeed be translated as "to dedicate." The latter carries the meaning "to consecrate" and could also signify a spiritual dimension of the volume at hand, which not only honors the plight of "her companions in suffering" but also elevates them to a status beyond the ordinary. With this act she venerates all former inmates, those who survived—and who might read this book—but also those who did not. The preface, therefore, serves a threefold purpose: it establishes her authority as survivor and witness; it honors and remembers her fellow inmates; and it serves as an orientation for a general audience on how to read these primary texts. Ultimately, Else Dormitzer assigns her readers a central role in the meaning-making process. The written "pictures" come to live in the interplay between reader and text, and as repositories of individual memory, they extend to empathetic readers outside of Theresienstadt as they become part of a secondary witnessing process.

---

41 Young, *Writing and Rewriting the Holocaust: Narrative and the Consequences of Interpretation*, 37.

The poems "Do not give up hope!," "Lost Years," and "Finale" respectively open and close the collection. They create a frame in which the remaining poems are placed that does not only establish a causal chronological connection between individual texts but also creates a narrative of redemption—the liberation of the oppressed people of Israel through help from God. The readers receive all poems within this positive construct and with the knowledge of survival for the author. From the safe distance of freedom, they can now bring back to life the "pictures" from Theresienstadt without forgetting the texts' underlying tensions.

"Do not give up hope!," the first poem, sets the tone for the collection, its first two stanzas describing the bleak life in the ghetto, thereby generating early images of days filled with constant sorrow, worries, and pain.

> Our lives are now threatened
> By worry, sorrow, misery, hardship,
> Not a ray of light penetrates the darkness,
> Blow follows upon blow and agony follows upon agony;
> [...]
> The days' dreadful sameness
> Passes hopelessly by us,
> And we spend night after night without sleep,
> In fear and in tears;

The poetic subject is part of a collective whole, expressing a communal voice by using the first-person plural possessive pronoun *unser* (our). But the reader learns that hope does exist to escape this dreadful existence, continuously nourished by a reaffirming inner voice: "Yet a voice inside speaks: / 'Do not give up hope, do not give up hope!'" The last stanza focuses entirely on revealing the source of strength, and it becomes apparent that it is the unshakable faith in God. This lasting belief is a source of optimism that will, one day, bear the fruits of liberty. In this manner, the poetic subject is trying to not only encourage itself but also others to remain vigilant in the face of darkness.

> He will stop the pain and the suffering,
> And set us free from the grip of our enemies,
> He blesses us with peace, freedom, light,
> Therefore, oh heart, do not give up hope!

The soothing mode of this poem, which extends to its formal realization, is easily detectable. The precise and clear language, simple rhyme scheme, and meter provide comfort and support as the poem provides a general depiction of the poetic subject's experience. Repetition marks individual stanzas, particularly that of the inner voice, speaking directly and clearly to an anonymous whole, encouraging the group not to despair. It is easy to see how the simple structure of the poem would lend itself to communal use and how a performance could have the capability to soothe the pain, at least temporarily. Thus, the modes of this first poem can be described as lyrical and spiritual, its functions as performance or even prayer, all providing communal and individual sustenance.

In the second poem, "Lost Years," the collective again laments the deprivations of the present moment, highlighting, in particular, the separation from loved ones and fear for their wellbeing. However, unlike the first poem, this time, the collective is turning directly to God to call for help:

> Where are you, children, parents, sisters, brothers?
> [...]
> We do not know where we may find you,
> We have been given no greeting written by your hands.
> We are wondering, anxiously: "Are you still alive?"
> And our eyes are filled with bitter tears.
> [...]
> What gives us the strength to endure all this?
> The hope, Lord and God, for Your mercy!
> Help your ill-fated, suffering people
> And lead us soon to better, brighter days.

But hope is a fragile concept, and, as the last poem, "Finale," illustrates, the collective voice has gone silent after years of imprisonment and anguish. However, then, at last, a miracle does happen:

> A day like any other, bleak and empty,
> Not a spark of hope is left in our hearts;
> The endless hours spent toiling,
> Interrupted only by a meager meal.
> As always, we fall into bed deeply disheartened

And close our tired eyes.
In the morning, ha!, a miracle has happened:
We see foreign uniforms all around,
It's the Russians, who are here to free us from the yoke,
Everywhere there is laughter, crying, cheering, yelling,
We rub our eyes to see if it is just a beautiful dream
That will soon burst like a soap bubble?
No, it is real! The nightmare is over.
O happiness, O bliss—we are going home!
We stand at the beginning of better times,
To you, oh Eternal One, we are grateful.
We praise You, with all of our hearts and souls.
You have come to rescue Your Children of Israel!

The tone of this poem transforms from one of despair and disbelief to that of exhilaration and praise. The past is immediately perceived as an uncanny nightmarish episode, and the poetic subject, again a communal voice ("*wir*"), instantaneously sees the beginning of new and better times. There is no room for further reflection as to what this future might look like, but the poem makes clear who is ultimately responsible for granting freedom, thus praising God. Written from within the events, the poem highlights freedom itself, a concept that naturally remains vague, and the poem's title, "Finale," underlines the conclusiveness of the end of suffering on the day of liberation. For the moment, the experience is joyful and represented as such. Like the collection's opening poem, "Finale" displays a spiritual mode by being designed as a poem of praise. While Else Dormitzer employs a rhyme scheme, it is not as regular as in "Do not Despair!," and the poem also lacks some of the lyrical characteristics of the first, for instance, repetition of words or organization in stanzas. It might, therefore, lend itself less for performance and certainly is a different realization than the first.

Dormitzer places "Finale" at the end of her collection, and the volume thus ends on a positive note. Arranging and sequencing the poems within a narrative of redemption provides her the opportunity to structure the experienced chronologically and causally, allowing her, in retrospect, to give meaning to past experience, to make some sense of it all, and to attempt creating closure for herself on paper. Shortly after the war, this affirmative interpretation of the past is not an exception; it can also be found in letters, diaries,

and chronicles. But the trauma of persecution, escape, and mass murder is difficult, if not impossible, to process, and closure can hardly be attained. Many survivors cannot return "home" because it is irrevocably lost. "Better times" come to be characterized by mourning, despair, anger, anxiety, desperation, and survivor's guilt. Continuing to live, as Ruth Klüger shows in her autobiography, is hard work, and for some survivors, it is simply impossible. Therefore, poetic texts displaying abstract and fragmented forms now appear more adequate for representing the ruptures of the immediate past than versified stanzas and traditional metaphorical language. "Rhyme and meter," observes lyricist Rose Ausländer:

> [...] collapsed in the aftermath, in the shock of survival, which we suffered belatedly. Flowery words wilted. Many nouns also became questionable in a mechanized world that belonged to the "man without qualities," the de-personalized human. The old vocabulary had to be exchanged.[42]

Else Dormitzer inserts the remaining seven poems within the narrative of redemption created by the opening and closing poems, thereby shedding light on additional aspects of everyday life in Theresienstadt. The reader learns about six recurring and concrete themes of daily life through her poetry: hunger, work, death, vermin, torture, and deportation. She writes about the hard, long workdays and laborious tasks in the mica workshop ("Mica"), for example, and satirically illustrates how the plague of insects robs prisoners of their minds and sleep every night ("The Night of the Bedbug"). "Unbearable, the ubiquitous vermin," Dormitzer characterizes the situation in her post-war testimonial,

> (fleas, lice, bedbugs, the latter in unimaginable quantities— once, I killed 103 in a single night in my bed, had to crush 40–50 of them sitting on the walls every morning, and slept for many weeks on the stone floor in the hallway, because it was more tolerable there). They tried to act aggressively against the plague of lice, because they carried epidemic typhus, the de-lousing procedure was among the worst inconveniences. The bedbugs were indestructible, and as

---

42   Ausländer, "Alles kann Motiv sein," 286.

common in the hospitals as in all other quarters, the only way to kill them would have been to set fire to all four corners of Th.

Like the poem "Finale," the poem "Census" describes a specific day in the camp's history, November 11, 1943. Here, Else Dormitzer inserts a short prose description before the poem to contextualize the specific event within the history of Theresienstadt. This day constitutes a "new method of torture" on which Camp Commandant Anton Burger instructs counting all prisoners in an extended roll call. "Some irregularities in the assessment of numbers," writes Emil Utitz, "led to the grotesque idea to hold a general census on an open field."[43] "Census" is the longest poem of the collection. In eight stanzas, she chronicles the tortuous events of the day, the endless hours of waiting for young and old, without food and water before being able to return "home" to the ghetto. "Old people were lying on the ground unconscious," she notes in her testimonial account, "starving children were crying, desperate men and women all around, until, to great relief, the order to return to the ghetto was finally given at nightfall." "The chosen people," as suggested by the repeated line of the poem, "shall be counted today."[44]

> Many hours pass! Those whose backs, hearts,
> And legs are failing sit on the hard dirt.
> Many start to feel weaker and weaker
> And, losing consciousness, drop to the ground.
> There they lie sprawled, as if their souls had faded away—
> The chosen people shall be counted today!
>
> The night falls, not a star on the firmament!
> On all lips, a burning question:
> "Will they make us stay her till dawn?"
> What trembling and foreboding, fright and worry!
> Thus, losing hope are even those whose faith is sturdy—
> The chosen people shall be counted today!

---

43 Mehring, *Ethik nach Theresienstadt*, 63.
44 Her poem lists the correct date of the census (November 11). However, her testimonial account mistakenly lists it as November 9, 1943.

In yet another poem, Dormitzer shows the agitation created by rumors of deportations and subsequent deportation announcements, describing the nervous restlessness of those selected to leave and of those staying behind. More than 87,000 people were deported to the East, of which a mere 4,000 survived.[45] "The worst of all horrors," she writes in her eyewitness account,

> were the transports leaving for Poland, usually consisting of all different kinds of people, old and young, sick and healthy, holders of the most important positions and people unable to work. The summons came in the middle of the night, those who were called had to go to "The Sluice" and could not come out again. They were not allowed to take much with them, they were driven down sealed-off streets by the gendarmes, and then at the train station loaded onto freight cars, packed tightly like herrings. On various occasions, some of their meager possessions were left behind at the train station when the commandant ordered the train to depart too soon, which was intentional of course. These kinds of transports carried 1,200–1,500 people, the transports in the fall of 1944 moved 15–20,000 people to Poland, many of them already dying.

As in other texts, Dormitzer succeeds in generating tension by transforming verbs and stringing them together as nouns in a series, thereby generating creative neologisms in the German language. Such a grammatical adjustment of turning verbs into concrete nouns—mostly verbs of motion and action—or combining verbs and nouns into singular nouns maximizes expression within short verses. This creative linguistic arrangement also adds concreteness as the new nouns articulate actions and feelings more effectively and broadly.

> A murmur, a whisper, an anxious plea
> In dark December days,
> Here a loud lament, there a quiet weeping,
> The whole city is on its feet,
> With just one word on everyone's lips:
>   Transport!

---

45 Hájková, *The Last Ghetto*, 9.

An icy breeze blows through the streets,
For the last time we hear: "Grab some bread!"
Our sheets are flapping, our beds are rolling,
We are packing our bags, our friends are offering
to help, before we must head off to The Sluice:
       Transport!

Consisting of four stanzas in total, the poem ends with fearful questions by those left behind and the appeal to God to keep them from the same fate. Dark descriptions of nature create an uncanny atmosphere, expressed in particular by the appearance of the grim reaper as personified death. Waiting patiently for his turn to take the living, he is the one constant companion of prisoners wherever they might go.

Now the time has come—a glance back to say farewell,
A last handshake, a good-luck-wish!
There stands the Reaper, he's brought his scythe,
He does not waver and he is here to stay,
He travels with you, wherever you go:
       Transport!

In Theresienstadt itself, the cause of most deaths is illness and disease caused by malnutrition. Here again, Else Dormitzer provides further information in her post-war testimony.

Indescribable the hunger that tormented the town in all those years. To illustrate: a normal person requires 2,400 calories per day, we received 1,200. Daily rations: *ersatz*-coffee in the morning, 0.3 liters of soup at lunch (green, watery, sometimes with soda), 270–320 grams of potatoes, among them many rotten ones, with one tablespoon of sauce or hash, every now and then a slice of sausage or a small piece of meat (often not fresh), alternatively a small portion of noodles, barley, or a small yeast dumpling with sauce in place of the potato, or a small flour dumpling. In the evening, 0.4 liters of soup, slightly thicker than at lunchtime. Also, one kilogram of bread to last three days. This also had to suffice for two dinners since twice for dinner there was only coffee. As a weekly ration we received sixty grams of butter, margarine, or some

spicy spread. Never eggs, fish, butter, cheese, fruit, vegetables, etc. Vegetables we had a few times in the months before liberation. The results of this kind of nutrition were bone softening and hunger edemas, which often caused the death of those who were afflicted. [...] About hygiene: our bread was brought to us on hearses and carried into the houses in a most unhygienic way.

To receive additional rations of food, prisoners often stand in lines for a chance of getting a second helping, a word that H. G. Adler records in his list of Theresienstadt-specific words as "reinforcements" (*Nachschub*): "From the Austrian military language for additionally distributed food after all portions were handed out. In other camps they had a second helpings [...]."[46] In a poem with the same title, Dormitzer creates a vivid linguistic snapshot of people bracing wind and bad weather in the hopes of receiving an extra ration of food. As in "Census," she inserts a short explanation of the term itself, placing it right before the poem, "Reinforcements was the term used for the distribution of leftover soup. We had to stand in line for it for many hours—often to no avail." Her text describes such a failed attempt, illustrating the painful wait endured by the fearful "emaciated figures" in line who also have to suffer through additional abuse by shouting men:

> Once in a while you hear men shouting,
> They are the kind who satisfy their desire
> To feel important by using their authority
> To torment those who are waiting in line.

It is precisely this negative trait in character that is "the achievement of Theresienstadt," as Dormitzer concludes in yet another poem, "Once and Now," in which she laments people's physical decline along with their moral decay, holding a mirror to the face of the reader by addressing them directly in the second person singular.

> Once you were so well-fed,
> Now you are so thin,
> [...]

---

46 Adler, *Theresienstadt*, xxxii.

Once you were full of kindness,
Now you are cruel,
[...]
These are the many achievements of
Theresienstadt!

In "Reinforcements" the hungry prisoners are too weak and cold to be bothered by the aggressiveness surrounding them. Despite the failed attempt to garner an additional food ration, they are back in line the next day, enduring the same risks and hardships as before.

Another poem, Dormitzer's "Death in Theresienstadt," depicts the process of dying and physical decay while at the same time chronicling how the dead are disposed of in the ghetto. "Death and dying," she notes in her postwar testimony, "was a chapter in itself."

> Excellent doctors, well-known experts from Berlin, Vienna, and Prague cared for the ill who received a special diet, even medication was available for quite a while; in the last year there was none, however. Despite the outstanding medical care, thousands fell victim to destitution and infectious diseases, and the mortality rate was enormous, some days up to 150, on average 30–50. All the dead were cremated. Collective funeral rites took place every day for all who had died. No one was admitted to the cremations. I would like to mention at this point that all urns were loaded onto lorries and tossed into the Elbe River shortly before we were liberated, which was a moment that we did not anticipate. This was done to destroy evidence of how many thousands had perished here.

By employing the metaphorical figure of a flying soul, Dormitzer creates an intertextual connection to the well-known German poem "Moonlit Night" (*Mondnacht*) written by Romantic writer Joseph Freiherr von Eichendorff. However, she substitutes the subjunctive mood of the original with the indicative and adds the adjective "poor" to the relevant verse.[47] Through this alteration, she succeeds linguistically in expressing the transformation

---

47 German orginal: "Und meine Seele spannte / Weit ihre Flügel aus / Flog durch die stillen Lande / Als flöge sie nach Haus." "Mondnacht," in *Eichendorff Gedichte*, ed. Traude Dienel

from life to death after the physical decomposition is described in concise and precise language. Eichendorff's construction has lived on in German culture ever since it was first published in 1837; to bring it up here seems absurd and out of place. And perhaps this is precisely its function. Whereas Eichendorff's text exalts the romantic artist's experience of nature and beauty in the context of death, the construction of death as mass murder serves to distance Dormitzer's poem from the original. Death is a reality entirely devoid of any romantic connotations, it is a pitiful regular occurrence, and the body is quickly prepared for immediate disposal and stripped of whatever personal valuables might remain. Using a regular rhyme scheme (couplet) in the German original renders the poem even more unsettling. No longer human, the individual has become an object in the machinery of death, its useless shell discarded quickly. Thus, she deprives the image Eichendorff creates in the original of its intrinsic enchantment, rendering it *ad absurdum* within the context of the camps.

> Our breath reduced to a wheeze, short and timid,
> And the nights, oh, how long they are.
> Finally, death calls out: "Now it is over!"
> And the poor soul returns to its origins.
> They don't make a lot of fuss about it here,
> The dead bodies are quickly placed in position,
> They drop a wool blanket over the heads,
> And pilfer whatever they find on the body.
> Two hours later, without a sound or a word,
> They push the body on a cart to the "good place."

Else Dormitzer and her sister survive Theresienstadt. Several weeks pass until they succeed in getting in touch with family in the Netherlands, weeks in which no one knows of each other's survival. A few days after the camp's liberation Else passes on a postcard to an American service member in Theresienstadt, Sgt. Eric M. Lipman, who mails it to Hilversum upon his return to Germany on May 17, containing the following short note:

(Frankfurt: Suhrkamp, 1977), available at Spiegel Online Kultur, accessed October 4, 2014, http://gutenberg.spiegel.de/buch/joseph-von-eichendorff-gedichte-4294/46.

Dear Madam, I have just returned from a mission at the concentration camp in Theresienstadt in Czechoslovakia. On that occasion, the enclosed message has been handed to me and it is a great pleasure for me, to send it to you, in the hope, that you and your dear ones will be together again soon.

On June 7, 1945, the two women finally start the cumbersome journey back to the Netherlands with approximately 1,650 former Dutch and German prisoners. Lasting three weeks, it takes them through a Europe destroyed by war, including their former hometown of Nuremberg. Since the sisters are stateless and lack the appropriate paperwork, they are not free to go upon arrival in the Netherlands but are placed into a quarantine camp in Sittard, where their ordeal continues for another three weeks.[48]

We were checked in at night. Then most of us were taken to the nearby Lynbroek monastery. The Dutch were soon released while the emigrants stayed interned under the watch of armed Dutch soldiers. The food sent there by the Americans was tasty. My sister had a bad eye problem and needed to consult an eye specialist. The permission to do so could only be obtained with difficulty, and in the end my sister was escorted to and from the doctor's office by an armed soldier. One Sunday my daughter and son-in-law visited from Hilversum and attempted to procure my release.

---

48 Dienke Hondius, *Return. Holocaust Survivors and Dutch Anti-Semitism*, trans. David Colmer (Westport: Praeger Publishers, 2003), sheds some light on the circumstances of the repatriation of stateless Jews in the Netherlands, including in the Leyenbroek cloister (the name is misspelled in Dormitzer's original document). "Yet another group was in danger of ending up in Vilt, as is shown by an article in *Het Parool* of July 10, 1945, headlined 'Stateless Desperate.' A reception center in the Leyenbroek cloister, just outside Sittard, was holding approximately 140 stateless persons, all Jews who had lived in the Netherlands in 1940. 'They think they are as good as free.' This was not the case. 'At the repatriation office they found themselves surrounded by NSB, members of the SS, and other scum who were still impudent enough to taunt them. Their fear of being confined together with them in one camp caused them to resort to a tested device: they put their Stars of David back on.' The intention had been to send the men in this group to the camp in Vilt. 'The men went and lay on their beds and declared that they would not go. The order was withdrawn an hour later.' Two days later, *Het Parool* reported that all but 16 of the stateless Jews at Leyenbroek had been released" (ibid., 88–89).

They were rebuffed sternly by the Dutch commandant. This was repeated on the following Sunday. Only after we submitted a protest to the authorities in England did we get freedom of movement. At 9 p.m. on July 11, 1945, I left the monastery with my sister in a rental car. My children had made a considerable sacrifice to come up with the money for the rental car. We drove on country roads that were still damaged and reached Hilversum the next morning at 3 a.m. Several of my former Theresienstadt companions in suffering were stuck in Lynbroek for a while longer, until they, too, finally found transportation to their interim residences. This period of internment in Holland was a worthy conclusion to the years of suffering in Theresienstadt.

CHAPTER FIVE

London and Hilversum, 1946–1958

After being reunited with her family in the Netherlands in July 1945, Else spends summer and fall with Hildegard, Richard, and Henk in Hilversum before finally traveling to London in December of the same year. In February 1946, she extends her stay in the United Kingdom with Richard, Elisabeth, and Dora Rosenfelder in the hopes of accommodating the family on the mainland since Hilde is expecting the couple's second child. From then on until 1957, one year before her death, Else divides her time between both families, staying six months of the year in Hilversum and the other six in the Rosenfelders' house in Golders Green, a community in northwest London popular with German-Jewish immigrants.[1] In the post-war years, her immediate family grows, seeing the birth of several grandchildren and great-grandchildren, including Irene Haas in June 1946 and her first great-grandson, Thomas Runkel, in October 1948.[2]

Soon after arriving in London, Else Dormitzer looks to connect with the refugee community from Germany in Britain and becomes actively engaged in the work of the New Liberal Jewish Congregation at Belsize Square Synagogue, a congregation founded by German immigrants in 1939.[3] On April 13, 1946, she gives her first presentation, "Life in Theresienstadt," and

---

1 Hagit Hadassa Lavsky, *The Creation of the German-Jewish Diaspora. Interwar German-Jewish Immigration to Palestine, the USA, and England* (New York: Walter de Gruyter, 2017), 131.
2 Unless otherwise noted, quotes in the main text of this chapter are from documents in the personal archive of surviving family members. All translations, including secondary materials unavailable in English, are mine.
3 For further information on The New Liberal Jewish Congregation at Belsize Square Synagogue and its community, including the Leo Baeck Lodge, see Marion Berghahn,

other talks follow suit, including for the women's organization of B'nai B'rith (Leo Baeck Women's Lodge No. 510). She also organizes regular meetings for a group of survivors from Theresienstadt, in which H. G. Adler participates, and starts working on her three German-language testimonial reports. Until this day, they are preserved in the Wiener Holocaust Library, named after the former associate director of the Central Union, Dr. Alfred Wiener, who, after surviving the Holocaust, also lives in London and corresponds regularly with Dormitzer.[4]

When Leo Baeck celebrates his seventy-fifth birthday in London in May 1948, Else pays tribute to his life, work, and legacy on behalf of his fellow Theresienstadt inmates in a piece entitled "Remembrance of Terezín."[5] He thanks her personally for the warm contribution, returning the compliment to a woman who, according to his own words, "was an example for many" in Theresienstadt.[6] A few months prior, in November 1947, Else Dormitzer marks the milestone of her seventieth birthday with friends and family, the celebration lasting for three days. Greatly touched by the numerous congratulations and accolades she receives from friends and acquaintances all over the world, including a printed tribute in the *Aufbau*, she writes in a letter to family on November 18: "I really feel quite ashamed, this attention is too much […], but one does have the feeling that one did not live for nothing."

In the post-war years, approximately until 1951, Dormitzer once again starts seeking outlets for her writing, this time in both English and German. At least eight essays appear in the congregation's community newsletter *Our Congregation*, whose editorial team she assists, as well as in other publications, including the *Synagogue Review* and the *AJR Review*.[7] Her poetry collection from Theresienstadt garners positive reviews in the *Aufbau* and the *Wiener Library Bulletin*, where the book is mentioned alongside the work of Gerty Spies and Nelly Sachs.

German-Jewish Refugees in England. The Ambiguities of Assimilation (New York: St. Martin's Press, 1984), 167–172.

4   Dormitzer was also a supporting member of the library. See "Correspondence with Else Dormitzer, 26 May, 1952–3 October, 1958," Wiener Holocaust Library, 3000/9/1/347.

5   *Supplement AJR Information*, May 1948, included as a paper clipping in Else Dormitzer's notebook, personal archive. Written in English.

6   Letter from Leo Baeck to Richard Haas, personal archive.

7   For further information on the Association of Jewish Refugees (AJR), see Berghahn, *German-Jewish Refugees in England*, 156–167.

Fresh and unusual evidence of the indomitable strength of the human spirit is given in in several recently published collections of verse. It is the poetry of the fighting, the suffering and persecuted—poetry under oppression, in ghettos and concentration camps, poetry even in the face of the gas chamber. We feel that these verses are as "documentary" as anything the Library possesses.[8]

The focus of her post-war work now turns away from documentation of events and experiences towards remembrance; writing to disrupt post-war silence and oblivion now become central themes in her work. In a 1946 contribution entitled "Memories of November 10, 1938" for the *Synagogue Review*, for example, Else Dormitzer recounts the events of the November pogrom, sharing her and her husband's experiences in Nuremberg with vivid descriptions, ending the piece with a call for continued remembrance: "Even in these rapidly moving times, we can never forget this night."[9] On the fifth anniversary of the liberation of Theresienstadt, she publishes the piece "Theresienstadt Five Years Ago" for the *AJR Review*, recounting the events of May 8, 1945, that ended the nightmare of internment. Shortly after Purim 1949, a spring holiday "marking the deliverance of the Jews from a royal death decree," she publishes another essay for the *Synagogue Review*, "Remember Amalek: Thoughts after Purim," in which she illustrates how the horror of the past cannot and should not be forgotten despite the well-meaning advice of others.[10] Beginning and closing the piece are specific cultural and political references that express her familiarity with British life, and more importantly, reflect immense gratitude towards the warm welcome she and her family receive in the United Kingdom, one echoed by numerous German immigrants in the 1930s and 1940s.[11]

---

8   *Wiener Library Bulletin*, September 1947, included as a paper clipping in Else Dormitzer's notebook, personal archive. Written in English.
9   *Synagogue Review*, November 1948, included as a paper clipping in Else Dormitzer's notebook, personal archive. Written in English.
10 "Purim," Holocaust Encyclopedia, accessed August 4, 2022: https://encyclopedia.ushmm.org/content/en/article/purim.
11 See Anthony Grenville's publication for the Association of Jewish Refugees, *Continental Britons. Jewish Refugees from Nazi Europe*, accessed July 3, 2022, https://ajr.org.uk/wp-content/uploads/2021/07/Continental-Britons-web-friendly-PDF.pdf.

One of Jerome K. Jerome's stories contains an incident of the horrible strangulation of a young woman by a snake—the memory of which haunted the broken widower ever after. When a friend once asked him, "Why do you recall these scenes?" he replied, "Recall them? They are always present in my mind". I am always reminded of this story, when after relating the terrible time in a Concentration Camp, I am asked. "Why don't you try to forget all these horrid things? Why don't you think of Lord Lytton's words: 'It is wisdom to forget and madness to remember?'" But I cannot accept Lord Lytton's philosophy, nor the well-meant advice of my friends. Like the hero in Jerome's novel, I constantly see the pictures from the past. [...] Such things one cannot forget. Nor does one want to forget them. They must be brought to the notion of everyone, in our fast moving days, particularly to those who seem to forget much too soon, and to those who don't want to hear. No one would wish to spoil the pleasure of those whom a lucky fate has spared such experiences. [...] And in this respect I think especially of Great Britain. She gave refuge, livelihood and civil rights to thousands of refugees, who thus were able to regain their faith in humanity. All who have escaped to these isles will forever remember with gratitude how much the British Government and the British people have done for them. The feeling of those who came here as foreigners and who with heart and soul are now devoted to their new home, are feelings of deep and eternal gratitude: thanks to England—God bless her.[12]

Enthusiastically, Else Dormitzer takes advantage of the easing of restrictions of the post-war years by the British government that permit naturalization for Jewish refugees, filing her application with the Home Office and officially becoming a citizen in 1951.[13]

---

12 *Synagogue Review*, May 1949, included as a paper clipping in Else Dormitzer's notebook, personal archive. Written in English.
13 Grenville, *Continental Britons*, 50–57.

Augustus 1957. 13. Cricklewood Rd. London n.w. 2. England.

Dormitzer & Rosenfelder & Co.

THOMAS RUNKEL.

Else Dormitzer (sitting) with family members in London, August 1957.

In 1946, Else's granddaughter Dora and her husband Rolf Runkel return to Germany from the United Kingdom. However, it is not until the early 1950s that Else visits her country of birth for a prolonged period, the first time since escaping the Nazi terror in 1939. Shortly after her seventy-fifth birthday in 1952, she travels to Fürth and Nuremberg, spending several days in Franconia, during which she also memorializes her husband Sigmund and his brother Louis. At the old Jewish cemetery on *Bärenschanzstraße* in Nuremberg, she organizes the inscription of their names on the original tombstone of her parents-in-law Jeanette and Philipp Dormitzer, along with the addition "both died in the Theresienstadt Concentration Camp." Until 1957, she repeats these annual visits to her hometown, at times combining her trips to Franconia with short stays in the nearby spa town of Bad Kissingen. In July 1953, she also travels to Switzerland for a public presentation at the refugee center *Les Berges du Léman* in Vevey, where she speaks in front of a primarily female audience, among them former acquaintances from Theresienstadt.

After a short illness, only a few months before her eighty-first birthday, Else Dormitzer dies in the German hospital in Hackney on June 3, 1958, the family heeding her last wish for cremation at Golders Green Crematorium. The obituary in the congregation's newsletter heralds her contributions

regarding female participation and representation in Jewish organizations one last time, aptly memorializing her accomplishments for generations to come.

> Her death breaks yet another physical link with the achievements of German Jewry. Mrs. Dormitzer will be remembered for her pioneering activities in the area of women's participation in the administration of Jewish organizations, and for the publications and lectures on her ideals of Jewish womanhood. [...] The physical link is broken, but the ideals for which she stood shall live on. *Sichronom livrocho*—may the memory of this splendid woman be a blessing to us all.[14]

---

14 *Our Congregation*, July/August 1958, personal archive. Written in English.

Else Dormitzer's Writings

Translator's Note
by Cornelius Partsch

Translators are present in the texts they endeavor to translate as co-creators, and the purpose and the context of the translation affect the translation strategy. Thus, translation can be viewed as an act of interpreting, mediating, transforming, and re-creating a text that is variable in form and content. As a translator who is engaging with Else Dormitzer's writings from and about Theresienstadt nearly eighty years after their creation, I have opted not to attempt to re-create the rhymes of Dormitzer's poems in my translation while aiming for fidelity to form in other aspects, as poems are formal utterances. This procedure differs from Ruth Schwertfeger's, who has contributed the only other translation of select poems to date, published in *Women of Theresienstadt* (1989). Schwertfeger's decision to craft a rhymed translation results in her making significant alterations to the original texts, both syntactically and semantically.

In not placing a primary and controlling focus on rhyme, I aim for greater equivalence between my translation and the original texts and to bring other aspects to the fore while also rendering the poems' gaps and ambiguities. It is my purpose to make possible a view of the context and complexity of the situation in which Else Dormitzer wrote her poems while also being guided by an awareness of a connection between textual features and an ethical attitude which is inscribed in Dormitzer's determined call for acknowledgment and remembrance of a time of catastrophe. Her poems, as well as the testimonial accounts, disclose the features of a shattered world, and their central purpose, as I would argue, is to describe the brutal and dehumanizing conditions in the Theresienstadt ghetto, to honor the suffering of those who were forced to endure them, and to bear witness for future times and readers.

Theresienstädter Bilder
Hilversum: De Boekenvriend, 1945

———————————

VORWORT

Euch, meine Schicksalsgenossen von Theresienstadt, sei dies Büchlein gewidmet! So oft ich Euch diese Verse vorlas, ertönte ringsum der Ruf: „Die Gedichte müssen Sie drucken lassen, wenn wir erst frei sind!" Ich versprach es! Nun sind wir frei und ich löse mein Wort ein.

Erinnerungen steigen in mir auf an die mit Euch gemeinsam verlebte schwere Zeit, da Hunger und Elend, Qualen mannigfachster Art das Dasein unerträglich machten, der Tod uns als Erlöser erscheinen musste. Solch gemeinschaftliches Erleben bindet fester als Blutsverwandtschaft, als jahrzehntelange Freundschaft von Jugend an.

Im Sinne dieser Verbundenheit weihe ich Euch die „Theresienstädter Bilder."

Hilversum (Holland) im Herbst 1945
ELSE DORMITZER

Pictures from Theresienstadt
Hilversum: De Boekenvriend, 1945

FOREWORD

To you, who were my companions in suffering in Theresienstadt, this small book is dedicated! Whenever I read these verses to you, you were adamant in proclaiming: "You have to get these poems printed, once we have been liberated!" I made a promise! Now we are free, and I stand by my word.

I often remember the difficult times I shared with you, when starvation and misery, and torments of all kinds made our existence unbearable, when we were forced to consider death to be our savior. Such a common experience binds us together more firmly than ties of blood, than lifelong friendship.

It is in the spirit of this bond that I dedicate "Pictures from Theresienstadt" to you.

Hilversum (Holland), autumn 1945
ELSE DORMITZER

VERZAGE NICHT!

Von Sorgen, Kummer, Elend, Not
Ist unser Dasein nun bedroht,
Kein Strahl durchdringt die Dunkelheit,
Schlag folgt auf Schlag und Leid auf Leid;
Doch eine inn're Stimme spricht:
„Verzage nicht, verzage nicht!"

Der Tage trübes Einerlei
Zieht hoffnungslos an uns vorbei,
Und ohne Schlaf wird Nacht um Nacht
In Angst und Tränen zugebracht;
Doch eine inn're Stimme spricht:
„Verzage nicht, verzage nicht!"

Auf diese Stimme ich vertrau',
Auf Gottes Hilfe fest ich bau'!
Er wird beenden Schmerz und Pein,
Uns aus der Feinde Hand befrei'n,
Er schenkt uns Frieden, Freiheit, Licht,
Darum, o Herz, verzage nicht!

DO NOT GIVE UP HOPE!

Our lives are now threatened
By worry, sorrow, misery, hardship,
Not a ray of light penetrates the darkness,
Blow follows upon blow and agony follows upon agony;
Yet a voice inside speaks:
"Do not give up hope, do not give up hope!"

The days' dreadful sameness
Passes hopelessly by us,
And we spend night after night without sleep,
In fear and in tears;
Yet a voice inside speaks:
"Do not give up hope, do not give up hope!"

In this voice I place my trust,
In God's help I firmly believe!
He will stop the pain and the suffering,
And set us free from the grip of our enemies,
He blesses us with peace, freedom, light,
Therefore, oh heart, do not give up hope!

VERLORENE JAHRE

Wer gibt uns die verlor'nen Jahre wieder,
In denen unsre Seele zagend bangte,
Das Herz nach Euch, Ihr Lieben, heiss verlangte.
Wo seid Ihr, Kinder, Eltern, Schwestern, Brüder?

Ihr, die mit uns in innigem Verbande
Zusammen lebten, bis ein hart' Geschick
Uns jählings traf, vernichtend alles Glück,
Und Euch wie uns entführt in fremde Lande.

Nicht wissen wir, wo wir Euch suchen sollen,
Kein Gruss von Eurer Hand ward uns gegeben.
Wir fragen angstvoll: „Seid ihr noch am Leben?"
Und bittre Tränen aus den Augen rollen.

Was gibt uns Kraft, dies alles zu ertragen?
Die Hoffnung, Herr und Gott, auf Dein Erbarmen!
Hilf Deinem Volk, dem unglücksel'gen armen
Und führ' uns bald zu bess'ren, hellen Tagen.

LOST YEARS

Who will give us back the lost years,
When our souls trembled with worry,
When our hearts, loved ones, longed for you desperately.
Where are you, children, parents, sisters, brothers?

You, who lived with us in heartfelt kinship,
Until a cruel stroke of fate
Suddenly befell us, laying waste to all happiness,
And took us all prisoner, away to foreign lands.

We do not know where we may find you,
We have been given no greeting written by your hands.
We are wondering, anxiously: "Are you still alive?"
And our eyes are filled with bitter tears.

What gives us the strength to endure all this?
The hope, Lord and God, for Your mercy!
Help your ill-fated, suffering people
And lead us soon to better, brighter days.

TRANSPORT

„Schleusse" ist der Ort, in dem die ankommenden
und abgehenden Transporte durchsucht und
ausgeraubt wurden.

Ein Raunen, Flüstern, ängstlich' Fragen
In düsteren Dezembertagen,
Hier laute Klag', dort leises Weinen,
Die ganze Stadt ist auf den Beinen,
In aller Mund ein einzig Wort:
　　　Transport!

Ein eis'ger Wind bläst durch die Gassen,
Zum letzten Mal heisst's: „Brote fassen!"
Ein Wäscheflattern, Betten rollen
Ein Rucksackpacken, Helfenwollen
Der Freunde, eh's zur Schleuss' geht fort:
　　　Transport!

Nun ist's soweit—ein Abschiedsblick,
Ein Händedruck, der Wunsch: Viel Glück!
Mit seiner Sens' steht Einer dort,
Der wanket nicht und geht nicht fort,
Er zieht mit Euch von Ort zu Ort:
　　　Transport!

Ein Ruf, ein Pfiff—es flattern Dohlen,
Wann wird man wohl die Nächsten holen?
Ist dies Geschick auch uns beschieden?
Wann winkt uns Ruh? Wann gibt es Frieden?
Beschütze uns, Du, unser Hort,
Vor dem Transport!

TRANSPORT

"The Sluice" is the place where the arriving and
departing transports were searched and plundered.

A murmur, a whisper, an anxious plea
In dark December days,
Here a loud lament, there a quiet weeping,
The whole city is on its feet,
With just one word on everyone's lips:
　　　　Transport!

An icy breeze is blowing through the streets,
For the last time we hear: "Grab some bread!"
Our sheets are flapping, our beds are rolling,
We are packing our bags, our friends are offering
to help, before we must head off to The Sluice:
　　　　Transport!

Now the time has come—a glance back to say farewell,
A last handshake, a good-luck-wish!
There stands the Reaper, he's brought his scythe,
He does not waver and he is here to stay,
He travels with you, wherever you go:
　　　　Transport!

A command, a whistle—the birds scatter in a great flutter of wings,
When will they come to take away the next group?
Are we condemned to the same fate?
When will we find calm? When will there be peace?
Protect us, You, our refuge,
From the Transport!

NACHSCHUB

*Nachschub wurde die Verteilung der übrig
gebliebenen Suppe genannt, für die man
stundenlang—gar oft vergeblich—anstehen musste.*

In Eis und Schnee, in Sturm und Regen
Begegnet man auf allen Wegen
Viel ausgemergelten Gestalten,
Die in der Hand den Blechnapf halten.
Sie woll'n—teils offen, meist verstohlen—
Sich Nachschub im Kasernhof holen.
Dort stehen sie in langen Schlangen
Und fragen voller Angst und Bangen:
„Wird es ein wenig Suppe geben?
Wir brauchen nötig sie zum Leben!
Erhält man sie auch ohne Karten?
In jedem Fall heisst's: Warten, warten!"
Man wartet nun in dumpfem Schweigen,
—Wie langsam doch die Stunden schleichen!—
Reibt sich die Hände, streckt die Glieder
Und stampfet, trippelt auf und nieder.
Dazwischen hört man Männer brüllen,
Die, um dem Geltungstrieb zu stillen,
Ihr Aufsichtsamt dazu erwählen,
Die Harrenden noch mehr zu quälen.
Vom Turm schlägt's zwei—die Hoffnung steigt!
Ob sich der Dampftopf endlich zeigt?
Da schallt ein Ruf von Weitem her:
„Es gibt heut keinen Nachschub mehr!"
Der Aufsichtsmann mit grobem Ton
Jagt die Enttäuschten rasch davon;
Die kehren nun mit stierem Blick
In ihre kalte Stub' zurück.
Und ist der nächste Mittag da,
Gehn wieder sie nach Golgatha!

REINFORCEMENTS

Reinforcements was the term used for the distribution of leftover soup. We had to stand in line for it for many hours—often to no avail.

In ice and snow, in storm and rain,
Wherever you go, you see them,
All those emaciated figures
Who are clutching in their hands a tin cup.
They are on their way, some openly, but most furtively,
to pick up reinforcements in the barracks yard.
There, they stand in long lines
And wonder full of fright and worry:
"Will there be a little soup left over?
We need it badly, to stay alive!
Can we get some even without ration cards?
In any case: what we must do is wait!"
All are waiting now in dull silence
—How long an hour can last!—
Rubbing their hands, stretching their limbs
And stomping, keeping their legs moving.
Once in a while you hear men shouting,
They are the kind who satisfy their desire
To feel important by using their authority
To torment those who are waiting in line.
The clock strikes two—it is a beacon of hope for us!
Will the steaming pot finally present itself?
Then an announcement is heard from far away:
"There are no reinforcements today!"
The guard rudely chases away
The disappointed crowd.
With blank stares, they all turn around
And shuffle back to their frigid quarters.
And when the next noon hour arrives,
They will once again go forth to Golgotha!

VOLKSZÄHLUNG

Am 11. November 1943 musste die gesamte jüdische
Bevölkerung Theresienstadts zwölf Stunden lang ohne
Speis und Trank im Freien stehen, um gezählt zu werden.
Da jeder Ghettoinsasse schon unzählige Male registriert war,
handelte es sich nur um eine neue Art der Quälerei.

Im Morgengrau'n durchziehen dichte Massen
Theresienstadts sonst menschenleere Gassen,
In Fünferreih'n sieht man in langen Zügen
Sie um die Plätze und die Ecken biegen.
Der Ordnungsdienst sieht nach, ob keiner fehlt—
Das auserwählte Volk wird heut' gezählt!

Man kann erblicken jede Art von Typen,
Denn nur die Kranken sind zurückgeblieben,
Man hat sie alle mit vereinter Kraft
Um 5 Uhr früh in's Siechenheim geschafft.
Der Lahme führt den Blinden, der sich quält—
Das auserwählte Volk wird heut' gezählt!

Gar viele Mütter schieben Kinderwagen,
Der Vater muss sein krankes Söhnchen tragen,
An Krücken, Stöcken schleppen sich die Alten,
Der Zählerdienst beginnt mit seinem Walten,
Aus Wolken sich die bleiche Sonne schält—
Das auserwählte Volk wird heut' gezählt!

Nun ist das Ziel erreicht! In weitem Bogen
Wird in den Bauschowitzer Grund gezogen,
Kein Stuhl, kein Stein und keine Bank zum Sitzen,
Kein Mäuerchen, den Rücken nur zu stützen,
„In Hundertschaften steh'n!" heisst der Befehl,
Damit das auserwählte Volk man leichter zähl'!

CENSUS

On November 11, 1943, the entire Jewish population
of Theresienstadt had to stand outdoors, without food
or drink, for twelve hours, in order to be counted. Since every
Ghetto inmate had already been registered countless times,
this was nothing more than a new method of torture.

At dawn, dense crowds move through the
Streets of Theresienstadt, which are normally empty,
One can observe them curving around squares and
Street corners in columns of five.
The Ghetto Police make sure no one has gone astray—
The chosen people shall be counted today!

One can espy all kinds of people,
Since only the sick stayed behind.
At five in the morning, they were all transferred to
The makeshift infirmary, in a concerted effort.
The lame is leading the blind, who is in agony—
The chosen people shall be counted today!

Many of the mothers are pushing strollers,
The fathers must carry their ailing sons,
On crutches or canes, the elderly are trudging along,
The census officials start their count,
A pallid sun is appearing in the sky—
The chosen people shall be counted today!

Now the destination is reached! Along a wide, curving path,
The crowd marches down into the Bauschowitz Basin,
No chairs or stones or benches to sit on,
Not even a small wall to lean against,
"Divide into groups of one hundred!" is the order of the day,
So that the chosen people may be counted more easily!

Der Mundvorrat ist aus, er war bescheiden,
Der Hunger wühlet in den Eingeweiden,
Nichts Warmes wird gereicht, kein Tropfen Wasser
Und Vieler Antlitz wird nun blass und blasser.
Wie hart, wenn Frost mit Mangel sich vermählt—
Das auserwählte Volk wird heut' gezählt!

Und Stund' um Stund' verrinnt! Auf hartem Raine
Sitzt, wem versagen Rücken, Herz und Beine!
So Mancher fühlt sich schwach und schwächer werden
Und sinkt bewusstlos nieder auf die Erden,
Dort liegt er ausgestreckt, als wie entseelt—
Das auserwählte Volk wird heut' gezählt!

Die Nacht bricht an, kein Stern am Firmament!
Auf allen Lippen e i n e Frage brennt:
„Wird man hier bleiben bis zum frühen Morgen?"
Welch Zittern, Zagen, Bangen, welche Sorgen!
Verzagt selbst der, den sonst sein Glaube stählt—
Das auserwählte Volk wird heut' gezählt!

Doch endlich kommt die Kunde—welches Glück!—
„Der Jude darf in's Ghetto jetzt zurück!"
Ein Hasten, Schieben, Drängen, Stossen, Fluchen,
Die Eltern Kinder, Kinder Eltern suchen.
Dann geht's nach Haus und keiner sich verhehlt:
Das auserwählte Volk ward heut' gezählt!

The food provisions soon vanish, they were modest,
Hunger rampages through the bowels,
Nothing warm is offered, not a drop of water,
And the faces of many turn a shade of pale.
How bitter when frost and dearth enter the fray—
The chosen people shall be counted today!

Many hours pass! Those whose backs, hearts,
And legs are failing sit on the hard dirt.
Many start to feel weaker and weaker
And, losing consciousness, drop to the ground.
There they lie sprawled, as if their souls had faded away—
The chosen people shall be counted today!

The night falls, not a star on the firmament!
On all lips, a single, burning question:
"Will they make us stay here till dawn?"
What trembling and foreboding, fright and worry!
Thus, losing hope are even those whose faith is sturdy—
The chosen people shall be counted today!

But at last the news arrives—what a relief!
"The Jew may return to the ghetto!"
Hurrying, pushing, shoving, bumping, cursing,
Parents and children are searching for each other.
Then they all head home, yet no one can deny:
The chosen people were counted today!

EINST UND JETZT

Einst warst Du so rundlich,
Jetzt bist Du so schlank
Einst warst kerngesund Du,
Jetzt bist Du meist krank.
Einst warst Du ganz sorglos,
Jetzt bist Du geplagt,
Einst warst Du voll Mut
Und jetzt bist Du verzagt.
Einst warst Du so offen,
Jetzt steckst Du voll List,
Einst warst Du ein Gourmand,
Jetzt frisst Du selbst Mist.
Einst warst Du goldehrlich,
Jetzt bist Du ein Dieb,
Einst schätzten Dich alle,
Wer hat Dich jetzt lieb?
Einst halfst Du den Ander'n,
Jetzt sorgst Du für Dich,
Einst warst Du verlässlich
Jetzt lässt Du in Stich.
Einst warst Du voll Güte,
Jetzt bist Du brutal,
Einst schliefest Du köstlich,
Jetzt wachst Du voll Qual.
Einst warst Du so reich
Und jetzt bist Du so arm,
Einst warst du frisch-fröhlich,
Jetzt fehlt jeder Charme.
Einst warst Du ein „Jemand",
Jetzt bist Du ein „Nichts",
Einst warst Du blitzsauber,
Vor Schmutz Du jetzt pichst.
Einst freut' Dich das Leben,
Jetzt hast Du es satt—
Das ist der Erfolg von
Theresienstadt!

ONCE AND NOW

Once you were so well-fed,
Now you are so thin,
Once you were as healthy as a horse,
Now you are mostly ailing.
Once you were quite carefree,
Now you are anguished,
Once you were full of courage,
And now you are disheartened.
Once you were so trusting,
Now you are always leery,
Once you were a gourmand,
Now you are willing to eat junk.
Once you were deeply honest,
Now you are a thief,
Once you were respected by all,
Who loves you now?
Once you helped others,
Now you take care of yourself,
Once you were reliable,
Now you leave people in the lurch.
Once you were full of kindness,
Now you are cruel,
Once you slept like a baby,
Now you lie awake, tormented.
Once you were so rich,
Now you are so poor,
Once you were radiant,
Now you lack any charm.
Once you were "somebody,"
Now you are a "nobody,"
Once you were squeaky clean,
Now you are caked with dirt.
Once you enjoyed life,
Now you are sick and tired of it—
These are the many achievements of
Theresienstadt!

WANZENNACHT

Es gibt hier Plagen ohne Zahl,
Doch keine schafft uns solche Qual
Wie die der Wanzen, die die Nacht
Zu einer wahren Hölle macht.
Sonst—nach des Tages Last und Müh'—
Begab man sich zu Bette früh
Und dachte (war man auch nicht satt!)
„Jetzt kann mich ganz Theresienstadt......"
Man schlief rasch ein, vergass sein Leid
Und träumte von der alten Zeit.
Doch jetzt? Man greift zum Veramon,
Nimmt Sedormit, Pyramidon,
Schluckt eimerweise Quadronox—
Es hilft doch alles nichts, Du Ochs,
Denn pünktlich mit dem Schlage zehn
Musst in den Wanzenkampf Du geh'n.
Ein Jucken, Beissen, Kribbeln, Krabbeln,
Du fühlst die Biester an Dir zappeln,
Und hast Du zwanzig umgebracht,
Ein Heer von Hundert Dich verlacht.
„Was tun?" spricht Zeus—man rennt hinaus
Und schüttelt seine Betten aus.
Ein anderer, des Ekels voll,
Springt in der Stub' herum wie toll:
Der dritte isst verzweifelt Brot,
Sein Nachbar gar mit Selbstmord droht,
Doch keiner, keiner löst die Frag':
„Wie wird man Herr der Wanzenplag?"
Die Lösung erst dereinst gelingt,
Wenn Frieden uns und Freiheit winkt,
Denn sind wir glücklich erst zu Haus',
Adieu dann Wanze, Floh und Laus!

THE NIGHT OF THE BEDBUG

There are countless vermin here,
But none torments us more
Than those bedbugs that turn the night
Into a veritable hell.
Once, after the hardships and the labors of the day,
We went to bed early
And thought (even if we were starving!)
"Now this whole place can kiss . . ."
We fell asleep quickly, forgot our suffering
And dreamt of the old times, of home.
But now? We reach for the Veramon,
We also take Sedormid, Pyramidon,
down buckets of Quadronox—
But this will accomplish nothing, you fool,
For right when the clock strikes ten
You will be at war with the bugs.
Itching, biting, prickling, scuttling,
You feel these beasts scampering all over your body,
And if you kill twenty of them,
An army of a hundred more appears, mocking you.
"What to do?" asks Zeus—we run outside
And shake out our beds.
Another prisoner, horror-stricken,
Jumps around the room like a madman:
A third poor wretch just devours his bread,
His neighbor even threatens to commit suicide,
But not one of them has an answer:
"How do we defeat this bedbugs' army?"
The solution will only come to us
When peace and freedom reign again,
For when fortune brings us back to our homes,
We'll say "Adieu" to bedbugs, fleas, and lice!

GLIMMER

Glimmer ist ein kriegswichtiges Material, zu dessen
Verarbeitung ausschliesslich Frauen verwendet wurden.

Um vier Uhr aus dem Bett heraus,
Um fünf Uhr schleunigst aus dem Haus,
In Finsternis auf schlechten Wegen
Eilt man dem gleichen Ziel entgegen.
Da hilft kein Klagen, kein Gewimmer:
Es ruft der Glimmer, Glimmer, Glimmer!

Zweitausend Frauen, jung und alt,
Steh'n in des Frohndienst's Allgewalt,
In langen Schichten von acht Stunden
So werden sie geplagt, geschunden
In schlechter Luft, im engen Zimmer,
Das will der Glimmer, Glimmer, Glimmer!

Auf hartem Schemel ohne Lehn',
Kann man sie rastlos schaffen seh'n,
Der Rücken krumm, im Kreuz ein Schmerz,
Bald rasch, bald langsam schlägt das Herz
Und vor den Augen—welch Geflimmer!
So wirkt der Glimmer, Glimmer, Glimmer!

Fürwahr, die Arbeit ist nicht leicht,
Und wird das Pensum nicht erreicht,
So droht als Sühne neues Leid:
„Ihr habt zwei Stunden Strafarbeit!"
Schreit laut ein Aufsichtsmann, ein grimmer,
Im Ton des Glimmer, Glimmer, Glimmer.

Es fallen Opfer ohne Zahl
Bei dieser Arbeit, dieser Qual;
Man trägt auf Bahren sie davon,
Der Tod, er harret ihrer schon.
Der Ärmsten letzter Ruf ist immer:
„Verflucht der Glimmer, Glimmer, Glimmer!"

MICA

Mica is a material crucial in times of war.
Only women were used in the manufacture of mica-containing products.

At four out of the bed,
At five hurry out of the house,
In the dark, using torn-up roads,
We rush towards the same destination,
No use in complaining, no use in moaning:
Mica calls, mica, mica!

Two thousand women, of all ages,
Toil under the thumb of forced labor,
In long shifts of eight hours,
That is how they are worked and mistreated
In stale air, in cramped quarters,
As required by mica, mica, mica!

On hard stools, without a back to lean against,
You can see them labor unrelentingly,
Their backs are bent, pain shooting into the spines,
Their hearts beating wildly, or hardly at all,
And before their eyes—flashes and flashes!
This is caused by mica, mica, mica!

Truly, the work is not easy,
And if the quota is not reached,
The punishment is further suffering:
"You'll stay here two hours more!"
Shouts a supervisor, savagely,
This is the sound of mica, mica, mica!

This toil claims countless victims,
Done in by the exertion, they collapse in agony;
They are carried away on stretchers,
Death, it is already waiting for them.
The last cry of these poor souls is always:
"Be damned, mica, mica, mica!"

TOD IN THERESIENSTADT

Täglich wird das Antlitz blass und blasser,
Ständig steigt in Bein und Leib das Wasser,
Keuchend geht der Atem, kurz und bang
Und die Nächte, ach, wie sind sie lang.
Endlich ruft der Tod: „Jetzt ist es aus!"
Und die arme Seele fliegt nach Haus.
Umständ' werden hier nicht viel gemacht,
Schnell die Leich' in Positur gebracht,
Eine Wolldeck' zieht man übers Haupt,
Was vorhanden, wird noch rasch geraubt.
Nach zwei Stunden, ohne Ton und Wort,
Schiebt den Toten man zum „guten Ort."
Zwanzig Kisten stehen dort beisammen,
Wandern tags darauf dann in die Flammen;
Freunde und Verwandte rings im Kreise
Schluchzen bei des Kaddisch's frommer Weise.
Kist' um Kiste wird nun rasch getragen
Zu der letzten Fahrt im Leichenwagen;
Man sieht nach, bis er enteilt dem Blick,
Kehrt im Strassenkot zur Stadt zurück.
Eine Frag' beschäftigt Dich allein:
„Wann werd' ich bei solchem Schub wohl sein?"

DEATH IN THERESIENSTADT

Every day, our faces grow more and more pale,
Our legs and bodies afflicted by the dropsy,
Our breath reduced to a wheeze, short and timid,
And the nights, oh, how long they are.
Finally, death calls out: "Now it is over!"
And our poor soul returns to its origins.
They don't make a lot of fuss about it here,
The dead bodies are quickly placed in position,
They drop a wool blanket over the heads,
And pilfer whatever they find on the body.
Two hours later, without a sound or a word,
They push the dead on a cart to the "good place."
Twenty coffins stand there already,
Ready to be fed to the flames the next day;
Friends and relatives gather around, sobbing,
As they hear the pious chant of the Kaddish.
Then one by one the boxes are swiftly carried away,
For their last journey, on a creaking hearse.
We watch it move away until it disappears from sight
And return to the town on dung-covered streets.
A single, burning question occupies your mind:
"When I will be dispatched in this manner?"

FINALE

Ein Tag wie alle andr'en, öd und leer,
Im Herzen keinen Funken Hoffnung mehr;
Des Dienstes ewig gleichgestellte Uhr
Durch spärlich Essen unterbrochen nur.
Man geht, wie immer, tief verstimmt zur Ruh'
Und schliesst erschöpft die müden Augen zu.
Am Morgen, ha, ein Wunder ist gescheh'n:
Man kann rings fremde Uniformen seh'n,
Die Russen sind's, die uns vom Joch befrei'n,
Man höret lachen, weinen, jauchzen, schrei'n,
Reibt sich die Augen—ist's ein schöner Traum,
Der rasch zerrinnen wird wie Seifenschaum?
Nein, es ist Wirklichkeit! Der Spuk ist aus.
O Glück, O Seligkeit—es geht nach Haus!
Wir steh'n am Anfang einer bess'ren Zeit,
Dir, Ewiger, sei unser Dank geweiht.
Wir preisen Dich mit Herz, Vermögen, Seel'.
Du hast erlöset Dein Volk Israel!

FINALE

A day like any other, bleak and empty,
Not a spark of hope is left in our hearts;
The endless hours spent toiling,
Interrupted only by a meager meal.
As always, we fall into bed deeply disheartened
And close our tired eyes.
In the morning, ha!, a miracle has happened:
We see foreign uniforms all around,
It's the Russians, who are here to free us from the yoke,
Everywhere there is laughter, crying, cheering, yelling,
We rub our eyes to see if it is just a beautiful dream
That will soon burst like a soap bubble?
No, it is real! The nightmare is over.
O happiness, O bliss—we are going home!
We stand at the beginning of better times,
To you, oh Eternal One, we are grateful.
We praise You, with all of our hearts and souls.
You have come to rescue Your Children of Israel!

Else Dormitzer: Erlebnisse in Nürnberg, Holland, Theresienstadt und beim Rücktransport nach Holland (aufgenommen von H. G. Adler)

Mit meinem Mann, dem Geheimen Justizrat Dr. Sigmund Dormitzer, lebten wir in Nürnberg; ich stand im 56., mein Mann im 64. Lebensjahr, als die Ereignisse von 1933 eintraten. Mein Mann war durch zehn Jahre Vorsitzender des Nürnberger Anwaltsvereines und dann stellvertretender Präsident der Nürnberger Anwaltskammer. Seine Tätigkeit als Anwalt konnte er bis November 1938 ausüben. Ich betätigte mich im lokalen wie im reichsdeutschen jüdischen Leben durch Jahrzehnte hindurch. Seit 1922 war ich Verwaltungsmitglied der Nürnberger Kultusgemeinde und damit das erste weibliche Verwaltungsmitglied einer jüdischen Gemeinde in Deutschland. Auch an der Arbeit im „Centralverein" war ich aktiv beteiligt. Meine Funktionen übte ich auch nach 1933 aus und wurde nun außerdem Vorstandsmitglied des „Jüdischen Kulturbundes", in dessen Rahmen ich musikalische Feierstunden für die Jugend veranstaltete.

Meine jüngere Tochter studierte Jura und hat am 1.4.1933 ihr Staatsexamen im Nürnberger Justizpalast absolviert, als mein Mann dieses Gebäude nicht mehr betreten durfte. Nachher wurde er allerdings wieder zugelassen. H. bekam im August 1933 den Titel Assessor, nachdem sie noch zuvor magna cum laude zum Dr. juris promoviert worden war. Eine Rechtspraxis welcher Art auch immer konnte sie in Deutschland freilich nicht mehr ausüben und ging darum im Oktober 1933 nach Prag, wo sie tschechisch lernte und bei einem Buchrevisor arbeitete. Da in der Tschechoslowakei kein rechtes Fortkommen für sie möglich war, blieb sie nicht lange. Sie heiratete einen gebürtigen Aachener halbjüdischer Abkunft, den sie von ihrer Studienzeit in München her kannte und wanderte mit ihm

Else Dormitzer: Experiences in Nuremberg, Holland, Theresienstadt, and during the Transport back to Holland (recorded by H. G. Adler)

My husband, the privy councilor Dr. Sigmund Dormitzer, and I lived in Nuremberg; I was in the fifty-sixth year of my life, and my husband in the sixty-fourth, when the events of 1933 occurred. Over a period of ten years, my husband was chairman of the Nuremberg Lawyers' Association and then vice-president of the Nuremberg Bar Association. He was able to practice as a lawyer until November 1938. For several decades, I was involved in Jewish life, both on the local level and in the Reich. Since 1922 I was on the administrative board of the Jewish Community in Nuremberg and, with that, the first female member serving on the administrative board of a Jewish community in Germany. Additionally, I was actively involved in the work of the "Central Union." I worked in these positions even after 1933 and, in fact, also became a board member of the "Jewish Cultural Union." In that capacity, I organized musical ceremonies for youth.

My younger daughter studied law and completed her state exam at the Nuremberg Palace of Justice on January 4, 1933, at a time when my husband was no longer allowed to enter the building. However, he was re-admitted later on. In August 1933, H. received the title of Assessor, after she had previously completed her doctorate in law *magna cum laude*. Of course, she was barred from practicing law, of any kind, in Germany and therefore went to Prague in October 1933, where she learned Czech and worked for an accountant. Since it was not possible for her to advance her career in Czechoslovakia, she did not stay there long. She married a man from Aachen, who was half-Jewish and whom she met while studying in Munich. The two of them emigrated to

im Jahre 1937 nach Holland aus, wo die beiden in Hilversum lebten und dort auch den Krieg überdauerten. Meine ältere Tochter E. ist mit ihrem Mann und ihren Kindern rechtzeitig nach England ausgewandert.

Die judenfeindlichen Massnahmen vor 1938 wurden in Nürnberg mit viel grösserer Härte durchgeführt als wohl fast überall sonst in Deutschland, wie es in der Stadt Streichers kaum anders sein konnte. So durften Parkanlagen, Badeanstalten, Gaststätten usw. schon bald nicht mehr von Juden besucht werden. Dr. Otto Hirsch von der „Reichsvertretung" in Berlin war erst durch einen von mir veranlassten Besuch [in] Nürnberg davon zu überzeugen, welch unverhältnismässig drückendere Zustände hier herrschten als in anderen Gross-Städten.

Ueber die Ereignisse in der Pogromnacht 1938 habe ich der Wiener Library ein Manuskript zur Verfügung gestellt, hier will ich kurz meine persönlichen Erlebnisse schildern. Wir wurden zweimal hintereinander in der Nacht in unserem Haus überfallen; erst kamen etwa 15 SA-Männer, die uns schwer misshandelten und verletzten, sie zertrümmerten die Möbel in unserer Wohnung, zerschnitten die Kissen und Möbel und hausten vandalisch; nachher erschienen mehrere Banditen, drangen in unser Schlafzimmer und zerschlugen meinem Mann das Nasenbein mit einer Stahlrute, misshandelten uns beide barbarisch. Nach diesem Überfall wurden wir blutüberströmt auf die Straße getrieben und suchten in der Nähe einen uns unbekannten christlichen Arzt auf, der die Vorgänge nicht recht verstand, das Ueberfallkommando der Polizei verständigen wollte und sich überaus menschlich und teilnahmevoll zu uns verhielt. Um 3 Uhr nachts fuhren wir mit einem Taxi in das Fürther jüdische Krankenhaus, wo wir aufgenommen wurden.

Das Krankenhaus war von Polizei besetzt, die christlichen Pflegerinnen mussten sofort das Hospital verlassen, die jüdischen waren mit allen jüd. Einwohnern von Fürth nachts auf dem Marktplatz versammelt, von dort wurden die Männer früh nach Dachau verschickt, die Frauen und Kinder durften heim. Am dritten Tage unseres Aufenthaltes, als unser Zustand, besonders aber der meines Mannes noch schlecht war, holte man uns ab, damit wir unser Haus verkauften. Man brachte uns zu einer Nazistelle, die „Heim und Hof" hiess. Um meinem Mann, der sehr erregt war, das Aergste abzunehmen, trat ich als Hauseigentümerin auf. Wir mussten in einem Vorzimmer warten, und wann immer einer von den Nazis den Raum betrat, mussten wir stramm stehen. Das bereitete einem nichtsnutzigen Jungen so viel Vergnügen dass er immer wieder auftauchte, damit mein Mann, dem das schwer fiel, nur immer wieder aufstehen müsse. Es gelang mir, einen etwas menschlicheren Funktionär daraufhin anzusprechen, der dem

Holland in the year 1937 and lived in Hilversum until the end of the war. My older daughter E. and her husband and children found the right moment to leave and emigrated to England.

In Nuremberg, the anti-Jewish measures prior to 1938 were carried out with much greater severity than probably anywhere else in Germany. It could hardly have happened any other way in the city of Streicher. Jews were quickly prohibited from entering parks, public pools, restaurants, etc. Dr. Otto Hirsch of the "Reich Representation of German Jews" in Berlin was only convinced that the conditions here were disproportionately more oppressive when compared to other large cities after I had invited him to Nuremberg to see for himself.

About the events that occurred during the pogrom night of 1938 I provided a manuscript to the Wiener Library. Here I will give a brief account of my personal experience. That night, we were assaulted twice in our home. First came about fifteen SA men who abused and injured us severely; they smashed the furniture in our apartment, cut the pillows and furniture to pieces and behaved like vandals. Later, more thugs appeared, invaded our bedroom, and broke my husband's nose with a steel rod. They abused us both barbarically. After this attack we were driven into the street, drenched in blood, and went to see a Christian doctor nearby. We did not know him, and it seemed that he did not comprehend fully what was happening, since he thought he could call the riot squad for help. Yet he behaved in an extremely humane and sympathetic way towards us. At three in the morning, we took a taxi to the Jewish Hospital in Fürth, where we were admitted.

The hospital had been occupied by the police, and the Christian nurses were ordered to leave the hospital immediately, while the Jewish nurses were gathered with all other Jewish residents of Fürth on the market square that night. From there, the men were taken to Dachau the next morning, and the women and children were allowed to return to their homes. On the third day of our stay, I was still not in good health, and my husband's condition was even worse, yet they came to pick us up so that they could get us to sell our house. They brought us to a Nazi office by the name of "Home and Hearth." In order to save my shaken husband from the worst ordeal I acted as the owner of the property. We had to wait in an anteroom and had to stand at attention whenever one of the Nazis stepped into the room. This gave a worthless young man so much pleasure that he came back repeatedly, thus forcing my suffering husband to have to get out of his chair again and again. I was able to bring this to the attention of a slightly

Jüngling dann anordnete: „Den Juden da lass sitzen!" Schliesslich kamen wir an die Reihe, und ich stimmte mit „jawohl" in jeder Einzelheit dem Zwangsverkaufe zu, weil ich spürte, dass jeder Widerspruch nur verhängnisvolle Folgen zeitigen könne. Wie recht ich damit hatte, konnte ich später feststellen, als ich erfuhr, dass ein Vetter, der sich zunächst geweigert hatte, in den Zwangsverkauf einzuwilligen, halbtot geschlagen wurde. Unser Haus mit Grund hatte einen Wert von 150 000 RM, wir mussten aber alles für 10 000 RM hergeben, wobei noch der Betrag nicht etwa uns, sondern der Partei zur Aufbewahrung übergeben wurde. Viel später, als—ich glaube auf Veranlassung Görings—die Zwangsverkäufe amtlich revidiert wurden, bekamen wir eine kleine Summe zugesprochen, die uns auch wirklich nach Holland überwiesen wurde, wo sie uns gut zustatten kam. Nach dem Zwangsverkauf begaben wir uns im Taxi zurück ins Krankenhaus.

Mein Mann hatte nie eine Auswanderung beabsichtigt, weil er seinen Kindern im Ausland nicht zur Last fallen wollte. Jetzt aber beauftragte er mich, alle nötigen Schritte einzuleiten. Aber sofort nach dem Prozess, hatten unsere Kinder sowohl in Holland wie in England binnen einer Woche uns die nötigen Papiere besorgt und gleichzeitig schickten uns Verwandte aus Amerika ein Affidavit. Am 1.3.1939 reisten wir nach Holland. Durch die Verwüstung unseres Heimes hatten wir nur noch sehr wenig bewegliche Habe, unser Reisegepäck hatte einen Wert von rund 800 RM, doch mussten wir (abgesehen von der Reichsfluchtsteuer) 4 500 RM Steuer bezahlen, um diese gebrauchten Gegenstände mitnehmen zu dürfen. Aus Holland reisten wir weiter nach England zu einem längeren Aufenthalt bei unseren Kindern und kehrten am 1.8.1939 nach Hilversum zurück. Hier lebten wir bei unseren Kindern bis zum Einmarsch der Deutschen in Holland.

Beim Einmarsch wurde mein Mann wie alle Deutschen von den Holländern verhaftet, doch konnte ich ihn mit Hilfe eines holländischen Arztes und eines ärztlichen Zeugnisses aus der Internierung sehr schnell befreien. Im Juni 1942 mussten wir Hilversum verlassen und nach Amsterdam ziehen. Wir lebten in einer Pension. Die Zeit der grossen Deportationen in Holland hatte begonnen, über eine Sammelstelle wurden die aus ihren Wohnungen Abgeholten nach dem Durchgangslager Westerbork geschafft. Als uns Gefahr drohte, denn man hatte uns schon holen wollen, hielten wir uns tagsüber bei einer Bekannten auf, die im „Judenrat" arbeitete und dort ausgezeichnete Verbindungen hatte. Als es einmal besonders bedrohlich aussah, weil man uns bei Tag gesucht hatte, haben wir dort sogar mit einer von dieser Dame beschafften Bewilligung zwei Wochen lang geschlafen.

more humane official who then chastised the young man: "Let that Jew stay in his seat!" Finally it was our turn, and I said "yes sir" to every detail of the forced sale as it was presented to me. I knew that any objection would only have disastrous consequences for us. That my instinct was correct I learned later when I heard that a cousin was almost beaten to death because he had at first refused to agree to the forced sale. Our property was worth 150,000 Reichsmark, yet we had to give it away for 10,000 Reichsmark. And that sum was not paid to us but was instead given to the party for safekeeping. Much later, when an official audit of the forced sales was ordered—I think by Göring—we received a small sum. That money was actually sent to Holland where we put it to good use. After the forced sale we fetched a taxi and went back to the hospital.

My husband had never intended to emigrate, because he did not want to be a burden to his children abroad. But now he asked me to make all the necessary arrangements. Immediately after we sold our home in this way, our children in both Holland and England procured the necessary papers for us, and at the same time our relatives in America sent us an affidavit. We traveled to Holland on March 1, 1939. Because of the destruction of our home, we only had a few moveable belongings left, our baggage for the trip was worth 800 Reichsmark, but we had to pay a fee of 4,500 Reichsmark to take these used items with us (in addition to the Reich Flight Tax). From Holland we continued on to England for a longer stay with our children and then returned to Hilversum on August 1, 1939. We lived there with our children up until the time of the German invasion of Holland.

After the invasion my husband, like all other Germans, was arrested by the Dutch, but I was able to have him released from internment quickly with the help of a Dutch doctor and a medical attestation. In June 1942 we had to leave Hilversum and move to Amsterdam. We lived in a boarding house. The time of large-scale deportations had begun in Holland. People were taken from their apartments to a collection site and then on to the Westerbork Transit Camp. When we were in danger, since they were planning to pick us up, we spent the daylight hours at an acquaintance's place. She worked at the "Jewish Council" and had excellent connections there. One time, when we were in great jeopardy because they had come by to look for us, we even stayed at her place for two weeks. This was possible because this lady had obtained an authorization.

Wir verlebten vier weitere Wochen in der Pension, als wir vorgeladen wurden, am 20. April in der SS-Kaserne zu erscheinen. Hier hielt uns der SS-Offizier Aus der Fünten eine Ansprache, in der er erklärte, dass die Reichsregierung als besondere einmalige Vergünstigung für verdienstvolle deutsche und holländische Juden einen Transport nach Theresienstadt gehen lasse. Wer von dem Angebot mitzufahren keinen Gebrauch mache, dürfe auf keine Rücksicht mehr rechnen, das bedeutete Transport nach Polen. Von Theresienstadt selbst erzählte der SS-Obersturmführer Wunderdinge. So versprach er uns SS-Verköstigung und vollkommene Freiheit. Im Orte sei ein Kino, ein Kaffeehaus und derlei mehr, besonders wusste Aus der Fünten die schöne Umgebung zu preisen: „Die Damen sollen gutes Schuhwerk mitnehmen, weil man Ausflüge machen kann." Am nächsten Tag fuhren wir bequem in Personenwagen zu vier Personen im Abteil mit unserem Gepäck und 50 Gulden, die man pro Person bewilligt hatte, ab. Während der Fahrt verteilte die SS Postkarten, die wir an unsere Angehörigen schreiben sollten.

Ueber meine Erlebnisse in Theresienstadt erfolgen hier nur solche Einzelheiten, die in meinen anderen Berichten über das Lager nicht enthalten sind und auch sonst kaum bekannt sein dürften.

Wir trafen nach einer Fahrt von höchstens 30 Stunden am 22.4.1943 in Bauschowitz ein und mussten mit unserem Gepäck nach Theresienstadt gehen, wo man uns das Geld abnahm und auch sonst alles, was den Kontrollorganen gefiel. Ich war glücklich, dass ich meinen Medikamentenbeutel retten konnte. Die „Schleuse" unseres Transportes war in der Aussiger Kaserne. Müssig zu sagen, dass alle in Amsterdam verheissenen Vergünstigungen sich als Lügen herausstellten. Mein Mann und ich erlitten bei der Ankunft in Theresienstadt den typischen Einlieferungsschock, durch den man in seinem ganzen Wesen gelähmt wurde. Mein Mann vermochte sich nie mehr davon zu erholen, während ich mich schon am zweiten Tage zusammenraffte, da ich erkannte dass man anders im Lager nicht durchhalten könne. Meine erste Aufgabe war es, meinem Mann, der damals 74 Jahre alt und leidend war, eine Bettstelle zu verschaffen, damit er nicht in unserem ersten Quartier L 116 auf dem blossen Erdboden schlafen musste. Mit Hilfe eines von Dr. Leo Baeck unterstützten Gesuches an den „Aeltestenrat", das ich einreichte, gelangte ich zum Ziel. Trotz aller möglichen Sorge um meinen Mann konnte ich leider seinen Verfall nicht aufhalten. Er starb am 9.12.1943 an einem Hungerödem in einer Krankenstube der Kaserne E IIIa.

We spent four additional weeks at the boarding house and were then summoned to appear at the *SS* barracks on April 20. The *SS* officer *aus der Fünten* gave a speech there and declared that the Reich government had arranged, as a special one-time privilege, that deserving German and Dutch Jews be transported to Theresienstadt. Those who did not take advantage of this offer could not count on being treated with respect, meaning that they would be placed on a transport to Poland. The *SS-Obersturmführer* described Theresienstadt in glowing terms. For example, he promised us *SS* meals and complete freedom. There was a movie theater in the town, a coffee house, and other such places. Aus der Fünten praised especially the surrounding areas: "The ladies should take along sturdy shoes, because it is possible to go on walks and hikes." The next day we left, sitting on a comfortable train, four persons per compartment, in possession of our luggage and fifty guilders, which had been given to all travelers. During the journey the *SS* handed out postcards, which we were supposed to write to relatives.

I am including here only those details about my experiences in Theresienstadt that are not included in my other texts about the camp and are probably unknown to most readers.

We arrived in Bauschowitz after a journey of about thirty hours on April 22, 1943. We had to walk to Theresienstadt, carrying our luggage. There, they took away our money and anything else that appealed to the officials. I was happy that I was able to salvage a bag with my medications. "The Sluice" for our transport was in the Aussiger Barracks. Needless to say, all benefits we had been promised in Amsterdam turned out to be lies. My husband and I suffered the typical admission shock when we arrived; which felt like we were totally paralyzed. My husband would not recover from this experience, yet I pulled myself together on the second day since I recognized that there was no other way to persevere in the camp. It was my first task to secure a bedstead for my husband who was seventy-four years old at the time and ailing and to ensure that he would not have to sleep on the bare ground in our quarters L 116. Dr. Leo Baeck supported a request I made to the "Council of Elders," and thus I succeeded. Despite taking care of my husband as well as possible I was unable to prevent his decline. He died on December 9, 1943, of a hunger edema in an infirmary in the barracks E IIIa.

Von Mitte April 1944 an verbrachte ich zehn Wochen mit einem bösartigen Karbunkel am Hinterkopf in der „septischen Baracke" der chirurgischen Abteilung des Krankenhauses E VI. Die Holzbaracke, die von den Gefangenen erst in der Lagerzeit errichtet worden war, stand im Hofe zwischen den Kasernen E VI und E VII, also ganz nahe von den elenden Kasematten in E VII, wo man alte Menschen zusammengepfercht hatte, und auch ganz nahe von der Grossküche E VII, wo Tausende von Menschen verpflegt wurden, die sich auf dem Hofe zur Essensausgabe anstellen mussten. Das Karbunkel, an dem ich litt, ist durch eine Ungezieferinfektion (Wanzen) entstanden und musste mehrmals von einem tschechischen Arzte operiert werden, dem kein ordentlicher Verbandsstoff, sondern nur Papier und Zellstoff zur Verfügung stand. Das und die allgemeinen Bedingungen haben den Genesungsprozess wesentlich verzögert. In meinem Raum waren etwa 20 Personen untergebracht, die Aerzte und die Krankenschwestern waren tüchtig. Fast alle Pflegerinnen wurden im Herbst 1944 nach Auschwitz deportiert. Eine Patientin hatte eine besonders böse Phlegmone am Arm, die sich der Lagerkommandant Rahm eigens einmal anschauen kam. Eines Tages musste unser Zimmer binnen zwei Stunden geräumt werden, weil man dringend Platz für 27 Patienten mit Hüftgelenksfrakturen brauchte. Solche und andere Brüche kamen in Theresienstadt, namentlich bei älteren Personen, häufig vor und waren schweren D-Avitaminosen zuzuschreiben.

Mein Lebenswille, nur wenige Monate nach dem Tode meines Mannes, war während dieser Krankheit beträchtlich geschwächt, eine abgründige Gleichgültigkeit gegenüber allem bemächtigte sich meiner. Aus dieser Lethargie verstand mich meine Schwester zu reißen, die in jener Zeit aus Westerbork im Lager angekommen war.

Einmal wurde eine Frau mittleren Alters eingeliefert, die jede Nahrung ablehnte, weil sie nicht leben wollte. Wie man sich auch um die Kranke bemühte, so blieb doch alles erfolglos, sie von ihrem Entschluss abzubringen. Nach acht Tagen ist diese Frau verhungert; sie hatte wirklich nichts zu sich genommen.

Während einer Zeit von wenig über zwei Jahren, die ich in Theresienstadt zubrachte, musste ich siebzehnmal mein Quartier [w]echseln. Die Lagerinsassen in ständiger Unruhe zu halten, gehörte zur Lagertaktik und hatte den gewünschten Effekt. Jede Übersiedlung war mit Verlust an Eigentum verbunden; teils wurden Sachen gestohlen, teils mussten die Träger, die den lokalen Transport durchführten, mit Geschenken bedacht werden. In meinem ersten Quartier L 116 lebte ein Ehepaar mit einem Jungen von 14

Starting in mid-April 1944 I spent ten weeks at the "Septic Barracks" of the surgical ward in the hospital E VI because of a malignant carbuncle on the back of my head. The wooden structure, which had been built by the prisoners, stood in the courtyard between Barracks E VI and E VII, not far at all from the miserable casemates in E VII where they had penned up the elderly, and also very close to the canteen kitchen E VII where thousands of people were fed. In order to receive food they had to stand in line in the courtyard. The carbuncle I was ill with came about as a result of a vermin infection (bedbugs). A Czech doctor who didn't have any regular dressing material at his disposal, but only paper and cellulose paper, had to operate on it several times. That and the general conditions delayed the process of recovery considerably. There were about twenty people accommodated in my room, and the doctors and nurses were doing their best. Almost all the nurses were deported to Auschwitz in the fall of 1944. One female patient had an especially nasty phlegmon on her arm, and camp commandant Rahm himself once came by to have a look at it. One day our room had to be cleared within two hours because they needed space urgently for twenty-seven patients who were suffering from hip fractures. Those and other fractures occurred often in Theresienstadt, mostly among the elderly. They were caused by a severe vitamin D deficiency.

Only a few months after the death of my husband my will to live had been further weakened by this period of being ill. An abysmal indifference towards everything around me took hold of me. It was my sister who managed to tear me out of this lethargic state. She had come to Theresienstadt from Westerbork around that time.

Once a middle-aged woman was admitted who refused to eat because she wished to die. All efforts to help her were in vain, and she could not be dissuaded. Eight days later this woman starved to death; she really had eaten absolutely nothing.

I spent just over two years in Theresienstadt, and during that time I had to move seventeen times. To keep the prisoners in constant unrest was part of the camp administration's strategy, and it had the desired effect. Every move meant a loss of property, some things were stolen and others had to be given as gifts to the movers who carried our stuff to the new location. In my first quarters, L 116, there was a couple with their fourteen-year-old boy who was mentally slow and seemed more like a five-year-old. Nevertheless, this boy was the most capable potato thief I ever knew in Theresienstadt. His parents were quite proud of him. The whole family was deported to the east. When

Jahren, der in seiner geistigen Entwicklung einem fünfjährigen Kinde glich. Nichtsdestoweniger war der Knabe der gewandteste Kartoffeldieb, der mir in Theresienstadt begegnet ist. Seine Eltern waren nicht wenig stolz darauf. Die Familie wurde nach dem Osten deportiert. Als ich 1944 aus dem Krankenhaus entlassen wurde, gelang es mir nach meinem Wunsch, mich in der Kaserne E IIIa einzuquartieren, in dem auch die Tuberkulosenabteilung untergebracht war. Wie ich an anderer Stelle mitgeteilt habe, hielt ich in Theresienstadt 275 Vorträge, darunter auch oft für alte und kranke Menschen. Ich gehörte zu den wenigen, die sich nicht scheuten, in allen Stuben der Tuberkulosenabteilung vorzutragen, was mir den grossen Dank der Kranken eintrug. Sie griffen in ihre Brotbeutel und schnitten mir Scheiben ab, die ich annahm—so war durch den Hunger meine Scheu und Angst vor der Krankheit geschwunden. Da E IIIa nur für Nichtarbeiter bestimmt war, ich aber wieder meinem Berufe nachging, konnte ich hier nicht bleiben und wurde in die Kaserne H V verlegt. Hier wieder musste ich fort, weil Angehörige holländischer Transporte in C III wohnen sollten, das man im Jahre 1944 als „holländische Kaserne" bestimmt hatte. Als am 8.3.1945 ein Transport ungarischer Juden im Lager eingeliefert wurde, mussten die Holländer aus C III weg, und ich übersiedelte in ein ehemaliges Zivilhaus in der Bahnhofstraße (L 2), wo ich bis zum Ende blieb.

Aus den letzten Monaten in Theresienstadt gebe ich hier einige Einzelheiten an, die wenig bekannt sein dürften. An den Zahnambulatorien wurden Aufschriften angebracht: „Es wird nicht mehr plombiert, es wird nur noch gerissen." Die Kolonne des schwedischen Roten Kreuzes, die am 15.4.1945 die dänischen Juden aus dem Lager abholte, bestand aus 20 Autocars. Als gegen Kriegsende die Evakuierungstransporte aus Konzentrationslagern nach Theresienstadt kamen und in strenger Quarantäne gehalten werden sollten, brach ein Transport aus und stürmte die Lagerapotheke, wo alles geraubt wurde, was sich irgendwie verzehren liess. So wurde der Inhalt von Vaselinedosen aufgegessen, ebenso andere Medikamente verzehrt.

Durch die Massendeportationen im Herbst 1944 wurden alle Aemter und Betriebe des Lagers ihrer meisten Mitarbeiter beraubt. So wurde es nötig dass vor allem alte Menschen (alle Personen über 65 Jahren waren damals vor der Verschickung sicher) statt ihrer angestellt werden mussten. Ich kam im Oktober 1944 als Beamtin bei der Post unter und behielt meine Stelle bis zur Befreiung. Insgesamt arbeiteten hier in jener Zeit 26 Beamte, darunter 16 Frauen. 13 stammten aus Deutschland, 5 aus Holland, 2 aus Oesterreich,

I was released from the hospital in 1944. I managed, according to my preference, to be placed in Barracks E IIIa, which also contained the tuberculosis ward. As I have shared elsewhere, I gave 275 public talks in Theresienstadt, many of them for the elderly and sick. I was among the few who did not shy away from speaking in all sections of the tuberculosis ward, and the patients appreciated this greatly. They reached into their bread bags and cut off a slice for me. I accepted these gladly, the hunger was stronger than any sense of caution or fear I felt of contracting the disease. Because E IIIa was designated only for non-workers, and I was actually working again, I could not stay there and was relocated to Barracks H V. Soon I had to leave again from there because some relatives of Dutch transports were to stay in C III, which was designated as the "Dutch Barracks" in 1944. When a transport of Hungarian Jews arrived in the camp on March 8, 1945, the Dutch had to leave C III. I relocated to a former civilian residence in Bahnhofsstraße (L 2) where I stayed till the end.

Here, I am stating a few, probably unknown details about the last months in Theresienstadt. Notices were posted outside the walk-in dental clinics: "We will no longer do fillings, we will only pull teeth from now on." A convoy from the Swedish Red Cross, consisting of twenty vehicles, took the Danish Jews from the camp on April 15, 1945. When the evacuation transports came to Theresienstadt from the concentration camps in the final days of the war, they had to be kept in strict quarantine. Once, a group from one of the transports broke free and stormed the camp pharmacy. They stole everything that could somehow be eaten, such as the contents of Vaseline jars and other types of medication.

Because of the mass deportations that occurred in the fall of 1944 all offices and operations in the camp were robbed of their personnel. And so it became necessary to assign predominantly old people (people over sixty-five were spared deportation) in their place. I got a position as postal clerk in October 1944 and worked there until we were liberated. All in all there were twenty-six clerks working here at that time, among them sixteen women. Thirteen were from Germany, five from Holland, two from Austria, one each from Czechoslovakia and Denmark; in addition, there were at least ten mailmen. After a lawyer by the name of Kozower-Beren had been deported, the director's position was given to another lawyer, Henschel, who tried his best to do the job well. His deputy, who was actually our supervisor, was a Dr. G. from Berlin. He committed suicide after the war in Berlin. He was corrupt and clever about getting everything he needed for himself and

je 1 aus der Tschechoslowakei und aus Daenemark; ausserdem beschäftigte man noch mindestens 10 Postboten. Leiter der Post (nach dem verschickten Rt. Kozower-Beren) war der ehemalige Rechtsanwalt Henschel, der sich bemühte, seine Sache ordentlich zu machen. Sein Stellvertreter, unser eigentlicher Chef, war ein Dr. G. aus Berlin, der nach dem Kriege in Berlin Selbstmord verübte. Er war bestechlich, verstand es, sich alles, was er für sich benötigte, zu verschaffen und stets seinen Vorteil zu wahren. Pakete, die an Tote oder Deportierte adressiert waren, erhielten die nächsten Hinterbliebenen nicht mehr wie früher automatisch. Nur ein bewilligtes Gesuch konnte zu einem Erfolg führen. Bewilligt wurde es gewöhnlich nur dann, wenn es sich bei den Bittstellern um hübsche jüngere Frauen handelte, hingegen war es nicht zu machen, ein an den Mann adressiertes Paket einer verwitweten Greisin zu überlassen, das von ihrer Tochter an den Vater adressiert war.

In der Post legte ich eine umfangreiche Kartothek aller Verschickten oder in Aussengruppen tätigen Gefangenen an; eingetragen wurden die Namen, das Geburtsjahr, die Transportnummer und die letzte Theresienstädter Adresse. Auf Befehl der SS musste diese Kartothek gegen Kriegsende vernichtet werden damit niemals festgestellt werden konnte, wie viel Tausende von Insassen Theresienstadt hatte. Jeden Tag hatte ich die sogenannten „Avisos"—die Ankündigungen eingelaufener Pakete und anderer Postsendungen—zu bearbeiten; es konnte sich bis um 168 Stück an einem Tag handeln. Die sog. „Paketschleuse", d.h. die Durchsuchung der Pakete nach verbotenem Inhalt, wurde damals ausser von einem tschechischen Gendarmen und jüdischen Ghettowachtmännern durchgeführt, wobei sich jeder Beteiligte schadlos hielt. In den Kanzleien der Postverwaltung habe ich jedoch keine Funktionäre der SS gesehen.

Einmal ersuchte man mich, zwei Burschen, die 12 bis 13 Jahre alt gewesen sein mochten und nicht gut taten, als Gehilfen zu verwenden. Ich gab ihnen einen Stoss Karten, einer sollte seine alphabetisch, der andere nach Zahlen ordnen. Als nach einer Weile nichts getan war, musste ich feststellen, dass sie sich weder im Alphabet noch im Zahlensystem auskannten. Ich schickte die beiden auf den Hof spielen und habe diese „Gehilfen" nicht wieder erblickt. Das charakterisiert die Vernachlässigung der Kinder in den primitivsten Elementarkenntnissen, da Unterricht an die Kinder streng verboten war.

Nach Kriegsende schlossen sich die ehemaligen Gefangenen nach Landmannschaften, also nach den Herkunftsländern ihrer Transporte,

about looking out for himself. Packages addressed to deceased or deported people were no longer automatically delivered to the next of kin. In those cases, a request had to be made and approved. These requests tended to be approved only when the petitioner turned out to be a beautiful young woman. By contrast, an older widow could not count on receiving a package sent by her daughter and addressed to her deceased husband.

At the post office I put together an extensive card file of all deportees and all those who were assigned to work outside of the ghetto. This file contained the names, the year of birth, the transport number and the last Theresienstadt address. By order of the SS this card file had to be destroyed at the end of the war, so that it should never be known how many thousands of inmates were actually at Theresienstadt. Every day I was working on the so-called "avisos"—notices of packages and other mail items that had come in. This could be as many as 168 on one day. The so-called "package sluice," i.e. the search for prohibited items in the packages, was conducted by both a Czech gendarme and Jewish ghetto guards, and they all grabbed what they could. At the higher levels of the post office administration I never saw any SS officials.

Once I was asked to take as assistants two good-for-nothing boys who were twelve or thirteen years old. I gave them a pile of cards to be ordered alphabetically and numerically. When I noticed that they were not making any progress I realized that they weren't familiar with the alphabet and did not know numbers, either. I sent them out into the yard to play and never saw these "helpers" again. This episode showcases the neglect of children who did not have even the most elementary skills because teaching them was strictly prohibited.

After the end of the war the former prisoners formed associations of refugees according to their countries of origin. This arrangement was also reflected in the offices of the Jewish Administration. We German emigrants who lived in Holland were counted among the Dutch association of refugees. But the Dutch Jews were very unfriendly towards the German emigrants who were fluent in Dutch for the most part. The Dutch Jews accused us of being "responsible for the misfortune of the Dutch Jews." This kind of hostility was not limited to the regular prisoners but was also expressed by the Dutch officials in charge. We could see the effects of this even during the registration of the Dutch group for the transport home. First, they took those who were Dutch by birth, and the emigrants' turn came only after they had spent an hour waiting anxiously. The entire group consisted of about 1,650 people.

zusammen, was auch in den Behörden der Selbstverwaltung zum Ausdruck kam. Wir deutschen Emigranten, die in Holland gelebt hatten, wurden zur holländischen Landsmannschaft gerechnet, doch stellten sich die holländischen Juden sehr unfreundlich zu den Emigranten ein, die fast durchwegs holländisch sprechen konnten. Man warf ihnen vor, sie wären „schuld am Unglück der holländischen Juden." Diese Feindseligkeit beschränkte sich nicht auf gewöhnlichen Insassen, sondern wurde auch von den verantwortlichen holländischen Funktionären ausgeübt. Das wirkte sich selbst bei der Registrierung der holländischen Truppe für den Heimtransport aus. Erst wurden die gebürtigen Holländer aufgenommen, dann nach einstündigem bang erregtem Warten kamen die Emigranten an die Reihe. Die gesamte Gruppe bestand aus rund 1 650 Personen.

Am 7.6.1945 wurde die Gruppe aufgerufen, um ½ 8 Uhr früh im Kasernenhof B V zu erscheinen. Alle Holländer sollten mit einem Transport abreisen; nun wurden die Listen kontrolliert. Wegen Raummangel war es jedem nur erlaubt, einen Koffer mitzunehmen. Wer mehr besass, trachtete seine Sachen befreundeten Pragern zur Aufbewahrung zu übergeben, um sie sich später nachschicken zu lassen. Jeder, der Theresienstadt verliess, hatte Anrecht auf 1000 tschechische Kronen, die von der ehemaligen „Bank" des Lagers ausgezahlt wurden und als Abfindung für das Zwangsguthaben an „Ghettogeld" gedacht waren. Ich erhielt nichts, weil die Bank gerade kein Geld hatte. Auf dem Kasernenhof mussten wir viele Stunden warten und bekamen eine Mahlzeit. Schliesslich sollten wir in die „Kleine Festung", übel berüchtigt durch die vielen dort vollstreckten Todesurteile; einen Teil des Weges mussten wir gehen, wobei jeder sein Gepäck selbst tragen musste. Den Rest des Weges legten wir auf Leiterwagen zurück. In der „Kleinen Festung" wurden wir von französischen RK-Schwestern mit DDT desinfiziert. Dann wurde jeder namentlich aufgerufen, es herrschte eine arge Verwirrung, der holländisch-jüdische Transportarzt führte sich schlecht auf, und schliesslich verliessen wir um 5 Uhr nachmittags die „Kleine Festung" und Theresienstadt in grossen französischen Ueberfallwagen. Sie waren unsagbar überfüllt, wir mussten auf unseren Koffern sitzen und hatten Hunger.

Wir kamen durch zerstörte Orte und passierten Karlsbad. In einem westböhmischen Schloss übernachteten wir. Der Aufenthalt verlängerte sich, erst am 11. Juni fuhren wir mit Autos weiter, kamen jedoch auch an diesem Tage nicht über die deutsche Grenze, sondern nur nach einem anderen Ort in Böhmen, wo man uns in einem Kino auf Strohschütten einquartierte. Eine volle Woche mussten wir hier zubringen. Die sudetendeutsche Bevölkerung

On June 7, 1945, the Dutch group was called to appear at 7:30 in the morning in the courtyard of Barracks B V. All of the Dutch were to leave on the same transport; now the above-mentioned lists were inspected. Because there was not enough space we were allowed only one suitcase. Those who had more than that entrusted their belongings to friends from Prague for safekeeping and to have them sent by mail later. Everyone leaving Theresienstadt was entitled to 1,000 Czech koruna, money that was paid out by the former camp "bank" and intended to be compensation for the "ghetto money" we had been forced to deposit. I did not receive anything because the bank happened to be broke. We waited for many hours in the barracks courtyard and received one meal. At last, we were told to go to the "Small Fortress," a notorious and feared place in Theresienstadt because so many executions had been carried out there. We had to walk for part of the way and carry our own luggage. We rode on a hay trailer for the rest of the way. At the "Small Fortress" we were disinfected with DDT by French Red Cross nurses. Then each person was called by name, there was a lot of confusion, the Dutch-Jewish transport doctor made a scene, and we finally left the "Small Fortress" and Theresienstadt for good at five in the afternoon, cramped into large French squad cars. We had to sit on our suitcases and we were starving.

We passed through destroyed towns and through Carlsbad. We stayed overnight in a castle in western Bohemia. Our departure was delayed, and we then continued on in cars on June 11, yet we still could not cross the border into Germany that day and stopped for the night in a different Bohemian town. We spent the night in a former movie theater, sleeping on sheafs of straw. We had to stay there for a full week. The Sudeten-German population met us with hostility. Once we experienced a service led by an American Army rabbi. On the 18th we continued our journey in British autobuses. We drove through the Franconian Switzerland, and I knew that we would soon reach Nuremberg, but I did not recognize the pile of rubble that was once a city. I was not able to speak as we passed through. The buses took us as far as Bamberg where it proved difficult to find a place to sleep. On the next day, June 19, they loaded us into cattle cars. These were locked during the night and unlit. No arrangements had been made for people to relieve themselves. We were not allowed to use the water closets inside the train stations; there were notices warning of typhoid fever everywhere. Our journey took us to Frankfurt, then to the Rhine River where the train was stopped for many hours due to the large amount of rail traffic that was crossing the river on a temporary bridge. We traveled alongside the left bank of the Rhine to Bonn,

verhielt sich sehr feindlich zu uns. Einmal erlebten wir einen Gottesdienst mit einem amerikanischen Heeresrabbiner. Am 18. wurde die Reise mit englischen Autobussen fortgesetzt. Wir fuhren durch die fränkische Schweiz, ich wusste, jetzt müssen wir bald in Nürnberg sein, aber die Trümmerstätte, die wir durchquerten, erkannte ich nicht; ich konnte kein Wort bei der Durchfahrt sprechen. Die Autobusse brachten uns bis Bamberg, wo wir nur schwer Unterkunft fanden. Am nächsten Tage, dem 19. Juni, verlud man uns in Viehwaggons. Bei Nacht wurden sie geschlossen und blieben unbeleuchtet. Für die Verrichtung der leiblichen Notdurft hatte man in ihnen nichts vorgekehrt. Die Wasserstellen auf den Bahnhöfen konnten nicht verwendet werden; überall waren Warnungen wegen Typhusgefahr angebracht. Die Reise ging über Frankfurt, dann kamen wir an den Rhein, wo der Zug viele Stunden wegen des grossen Bahnverkehrs warten musste, der über eine Notbrücke geleitet wurde. Wir fuhren dem linken Rheinufer entlang bis Bonn, von wo der Zug unter Vermeidung von Köln über Aachen nach Maastricht fuhr.

Hier kamen wir am 21. Juni an und erhielten nichts zu essen, nur lauwarme Milch wurde uns gereicht, aber ärger war, dass man uns nicht entliess, wie wir gehofft hatten, sondern in ein Quarantänelager nach Sittard brachte. Hier wurden wir nachts registriert. Dann wurden die meisten in das Kloster Lynbroek geschafft, das in der Nähe ist. Die Holländer wurden bald entlassen, während die Emigranten unter Bewachung holländischer Soldaten mit Karabinern interniert blieben. Die von den Amerikanern gelieferte Nahrung war gut. Meine Schwester hatte ein schweres Augenleiden und sollte einen Augenarzt konsultieren. Die Erlaubnis wurde nur unter Schwierigkeiten erreicht, meine Schwester wurde hin und zurück von einem Soldaten mit Karabiner eskortiert. Eines Sonntags kam meine Tochter mit dem Schwiegersohn aus Hilversum, um meine Entlassung zu erreichen. Sie wurden vom unfreundlichen holländischen Kommandanten abgelehnt. Dasselbe wiederholte sich am folgenden Sonntag. Erst ein Protest, der nach England geleitet wurde, bewirkte, dass uns Bewegungsfreiheit gewahrt wurde. Am 11.7.1945 verliess ich um 9 Uhr abends mit meiner Schwester das Kloster in einem Mietauto, für dessen Bezahlung meine Kinder ein grosses Opfer brachten. Die Fahrt ging über weite Strecken auf noch zerstörten Landstrassen nach Hilversum, wo wir am nächsten Tage um 3 Uhr früh ankamen. Manche ehemaligen Theresienstädter Leidensgefährten waren aber noch immer in Lynbroek, bis auch sie Transportmöglichkeiten nach ihren derweiligen Wohnplätzen bekamen. Diese holländische Internierungszeit war der würdige Abschluss der Theresienstädter Leidensjahre.

and from there the train proceeded to Maastricht by way of Aachen, circumventing Cologne.

We arrived in Maastricht on June 21 and received no food, only lukewarm milk, but even worse was the fact that we were not released, as we had hoped, but instead transferred to a quarantine camp in Sittard. We were checked in at night. Then most of us were taken to the nearby Lynbroek monastery. The Dutch were soon released while the emigrants stayed interned under the watch of armed Dutch soldiers. The food sent there by the Americans was tasty. My sister had a bad eye problem and needed to consult an eye specialist. The permission to do so could only be obtained with difficulty, and in the end my sister was escorted to and from the doctor's office by an armed soldier. One Sunday my daughter and son-in-law visited from Hilversum and attempted to procure my release. They were rebuffed sternly by the Dutch commandant. This was repeated on the following Sunday. Only after we submitted a protest to the authorities in England did we get freedom of movement. At 9 p.m. on July 11, 1945, I left the monastery with my sister in a rental car. My children had made a considerable sacrifice to come up with the money for the rental car. We drove on country roads that were still damaged and reached Hilversum the next morning at 3 a.m. Several of my former Theresienstadt companions in suffering were stuck in Lynbroek for a while longer, until they, too, finally found transportation to their interim residences. This period of internment in Holland was a worthy conclusion to the years of suffering in Theresienstadt.

Leben in Theresienstadt
Von Mrs. Else Dormitzer, London
(September 1945)

────────────

Nun über das Leben in Theresienstadt. Wo soll ich da anfangen, wo auf-
hören! Als Einleitung, wie wir hinkamen: In Amsterdam nachts 12 Uhr eine
Depesche mit Vorladung zum S.S. Obersturmführer für nächsten Tag 12 Uhr
(17. April 1943). Dort Rede von ihm an alle Eingeladenen, dass die Deutsche
Regierung als besondere Vergünstigung für verdienstvolle deutsche und hol-
ländische Juden einen Extra-Transport nach Th. gehen lässt, all wo man unter
eigener jüdischer Verwaltung, vollständiger Freiheit, gleichen Rationen wie
die S.S., Theater, Kino, Ausflugsmöglichkeiten ein wahrhaft paradiesisches
Leben führen könne. Wer nicht acceptiert, kann auf keine Rücksicht mehr
rechnen (bedeutet Transport nach Polen). So willigte man ein, wenn auch
schweren Herzens, denn der Abschied von Holland, Verwandten und
Freunden fiel schwer. Die Fahrt im Zug (350 Personen) verlief angenehm
und nach ca. 28 Stunden erreichte man Bauschowitz, da die Bahn damals
noch nicht bis Th. ging. Sofort ein total verändertes Bild: Kommandorufe
und Geschrei, lauter S.S. zum Empfang, Abmarschbefehl für einstündigen
Marsch bei Hitze auf staubiger Landstrasse, beladen mit allem Gepäck (was
nicht mehr selbst getragen werden konnte, blieb am Bahnhof stehen), den
jüdischen Helfern wurde strengstens verboten, uns tragen zu helfen. Ankunft
mehr tot als lebendig in Theresienstadt. Die Einwohnerschaft auf den Straßen
versammelt, da die Nachricht von der Ankunft des 1. Hollandtransportes
alles herausgelockt hatte. Einzug in die „Schleuse" (Untersuchungsstation
durch die Deutschen. „Schleusen" als Zeitwort bedeutete dort „Stehlen," und
damit ist die Bestimmung des Platzes schon erläutert). Sofortige Trennung
der Ehepaare, Anstellen zum Gepäckuntersuchen von 6–11 Uhr abends
ohne einen Bissen oder einen Tropfen. S.S. Offizier schreit herein, dass
der sofort schiessen lässt, wenn nicht absolute Stille herrscht. Aus unseren
Koffern Entfernung sämtlicher Lebensmittel, Medikamente, Toilett-und
Schreibsachen, elektrischer Gegenstände. Abnehmen der von den Deutschen
Behörden in Holland genehmigten 50-hfl., Uhren, Füllfederhalter, etc.

Life in Theresienstadt
By Mrs. Else Dormitzer, London (September 1945)

Now about life in Theresienstadt. Where to start, where to finish! First: how we got there. In Amsterdam we received a dispatch at midnight containing a summons to appear before the *SS-Obersturmführer* on the next day at noon (April 17, 1943). There, a speech by him to all invitees: that the German government had arranged, as a special privilege, that an extra transport would be headed to Th. for deserving German and Dutch Jews. There, we could live a truly paradisiacal life, under Jewish self-government, in complete freedom, enjoy the same food rations as the *SS*, theater, movies, and many possibilities for recreation in the surrounding area. Those who did not take advantage of this offer could no longer count on respectful treatment (i.e. transport to Poland). So we accepted, with a heavy heart. Saying farewell to Holland, relatives, and friends was very difficult. The train journey (350 people) was comfortable, and we reached Bauschowitz after ca. twenty-eight hours because the train tracks did not extend to Th. in those days. Immediately a different scene: barked orders and shouting, lots of *SS* to welcome us, the order to start moving for the hour-long march, in oppressive heat and on dusty country roads, laden with all the luggage we could carry (everything else was left at the train station), the Jewish helpers were strictly prohibited from carrying anything for us. Arrival in Theresienstadt more dead than alive.

The ghetto inhabitants gathered on the streets since word of the arrival of the first transport from Holland had lured them out of their quarters. Entry into "The Sluice" (German inspection station. As a verb, "to sluice" here meant "to steal," and that says it all about the function of the place). Immediate separation of married couples, standing in line for luggage inspection from 6 to 11 p.m., without a bite to eat or a drop to drink. *SS* officer yells that he would give the order to shoot if anyone made a sound. From our suitcases, removal of all food items, medications, toiletries, writing tools, all powered items. Taking away of the fifty guilders given to us by the German authorities in Holland, watches, fountain pens, etc. All accompanied

Inzwischen Geschrei und Prügeln derjenigen, bei denen noch Geld oder Schmuck vorgefunden wurde und ihre Abführung ins Gefängnis. Ärztliche Untersuchung und Umhängung eines Nummernschildes, das von nun an quasi die Stelle des Namens annahm. Schlaflose Nacht auf harten Pritschen, erste Bekanntschaft mit Latrinen. Am folgenden Morgen Abmarsch in die Quartiere. Nicht die erwarteten und versprochenen Altersheime, für die unsere aus Deutschland gekommenen Glaubensgenossen daheim ihr ganzes Geld abgenommen bekommen hatten, sondern überfüllte, jeglichen Komforts entbehrende Räume, meist in Kasernen oder grossen Häuserblocks. Mein Mann und ich sofort getrennt, aber wenigstens im gleichen Hause untergebracht, je zu siebzehnt in kleinem Zimmer. Beide—wie alle anderen Insassen—auf dem Fussboden einen kleinen harten Strohsack als Lagerstatt vorfindend, weder Tisch noch Stuhl, noch ein Nagel in der Wand, noch Schrank oder Kommode. Die Essensabgabe mit langem Anstehen bei jedem Wetter in Höfen. Dazu immer gerade Ausgehverbot und Lichtsperre (für das Vergehen jedes Einzelnen wurde meist die ganze Stadt bestraft), was bedeutete, dass man einige Wochen im verwahrlosten Hof zubringen musste und vom Eintritt der Dunkelheit im Finstern sass. Alle häuslichen Verrichtungen, Putzen, Fegen, Waschen, musste man selbst verrichten, ausserdem galt noch die allgemeine Arbeitspflicht für jeden Einwohner, ob alt oder jung. Anfangs war dies 8 Stunden, später 10-Stundentag. Es gab weder Sonn- noch Feiertage, auch keine jüdischen. Die zu unserer Begrüßung gekommenen Besucher aus der Vaterstadt konnten wir meistens nicht erkennen, ausgemergelte Geripppe mit glanzlosen, starren Augen, gebrochene Menschen. Viele, nach denen wir fragten, u. a. unsere allernächsten Verwandten (Bruder, Schwager, Schwägerin, Cousinen) schon tot, einige davon durch Selbstmord geendet. Unerträglich das in allen Gebäuden vorhandene Ungeziefer (Flöhe, Läuse, Wanzen, letztere in unvorstellbaren Massen—ich selbst tötete in einer Nacht 103 Stück in meinem Bett, hatte jeden Morgen 40–50 an der Wand zu vernichten und schlief viele Wochen lang auf dem Steinboden im Gang, weil es dort erträglicher war.) Die Läuseplage wurde energisch bekämpft, da durch sie Flecktyphus übertragen wurde, die Prozedur der Entlausung gehörte zu den grössten Unannehmlichkeiten. Die Wanzen waren unausrottbar und in den Krankenhäusern genau so verbreitet wie in den anderen Quartieren, das einzige Mittel, sie zu vernichten, wäre gewesen, Th. an 4 Ecken anzuzünden. Nicht zu schildern waren die Hungerqualen, die die Stadt in all den Jahren zu ertragen hatte. Zur Illustration: 2 400 Kalorien hat der Normalmensch pro Tag nötig, wir erhielten 1 200. Tagesrationen: Früh Kaffee-Ersatz, Mittag

by shouting and beatings of those who still had money or jewelry on them; they were taken to prison. Medical examination and placing on the body of a numbered sign that from then on, in effect, replaced the names. Sleepless night on hard pallets, first acquaintance with the latrines. The following morning, march to the quarters. Not the expected and promised senior residences, for which our compatriots from Germany had been robbed of all their money, but rather overcrowded rooms, devoid of any kind of comfort, mostly in barracks or housing blocks. My husband and I were immediately separated, but at least housed in the same building, each with sixteen others in a small room. Both of us—as all other inmates—on the floor and finding there a small, hard sack of straw as a place to sleep. Neither table nor chair, nor a nail in the wall, nor wardrobe or dresser. Distribution of food with long wait times, standing in line in all kinds of weather, in the courtyards. Added to that, we always had curfew and orders to turn off all lights (if one individual disobeyed, they usually punished the entire town), which meant that we had to spend several weeks in a shabby yard and to sit around in the dark when night fell. All domestic chores, cleaning, sweeping, washing, we had to do ourselves. Also, there was general work duty for all inmates, young or old. At first this was an eight-hour day, later a ten-hour day. There were no Sundays or holidays, not any Jewish ones either. Most of the time we were unable to recognize the people from our hometowns who came by to visit and welcome us, emaciated skeletons with dull, staring eyes, broken human beings. Many we inquired about, among them our closest relatives (brothers, brothers-in-law, sisters-in-law, cousins), were already dead, some by suicide. Unbearable the ubiquitous vermin (fleas, lice, bedbugs, the latter in unimaginable quantities—once, I killed 103 in a single night in my bed, had to crush 40–50 of them sitting on the walls every morning, and slept for many weeks on the stone floor in the hallway, because it was more tolerable there). They tried to act aggressively against the plague of lice, because they carried epidemic typhus, the delousing procedure was among the worst of the inconveniences. The bedbugs were indestructible, and as common in the hospitals as in all other quarters, the only way to kill them would have been to set fire to all four corners of Th.

Indescribable the hunger that tormented the town in all those years. To illustrate: a normal person requires 2,400 calories per day, we received 1,200. Daily rations: *ersatz* coffee in the morning, 0.3 liters of soup at lunch (green, watery, sometimes with soda), 270–320 grams of potatoes, among them many rotten ones, with one tablespoon of sauce or hash, every now and then

0,3l Suppe (grüne, dünne z. T. mit Soda vermischt), 270–320 gr. Kartoffeln, darunter sehr viel faule, dazu einen Esslöffel voll Sauce oder Haschee, hier und da eine Scheibe Wurst oder ein Stückchen Fleisch (oft nicht mehr frisch), dazwischen eine kleine Portion Nudeln, Graupen oder eine kleine Dampfnudel mit Sauce anstelle der Kartoffeln oder ein kleines Mehlknödel. Abends 0,4l Suppe, etwas dicker als mittags. Dazu für 3 Tage ein Kilo Brot, das auch für 2 Abendessen reichen musste, da es an zwei Abenden nur Kaffee gab. Als Wochenration 60gr. Margarine, Marmelade oder etwas scharfen Brotaufstrich. Niemals Eier, Fisch, Butter, Käse, Obst, Gemüse, usw., letzteres manchmal in den letzten Monaten vor der Befreiung. Die Folge dieser Ernährung waren Knochenerweichung und Hungerödeme, die vielfach den Tod des davon Befallenen verursachten. Fiel jemand hin, so brach irgend ein Knochen, meistens waren es Schenkelhalsbrüche. Beispiel: das Zimmer, in dem ich einmal im Krankenhaus lag, musste innerhalb einer Stunde geräumt werden, weil 27 Schenkelhalsbrüche gemeldet waren.

–Unsere Behandlung von Seiten der Deutschen kann nicht verglichen werden mit der in Auschwitz, Buchenwald oder ähnlichen Konzentrationslagern. Wir Insassen hatten im täglichen Leben nichts mit den Deutschen zu tun, sondern standen privat und bei der Arbeit unter jüdischer Aufsicht (jüdischer Ordnungsdienst, Ghettogericht für Diebstähle, Ungehorsamen etc., Arbeitsgericht, Haus-und Stubenälteste für Sauberkeit, Ordnung und Disziplin in den Häusern). Ohrfeigen, Stockschläge, und Misshandlungen gab es natürlich bei gelegentlichem Zusammentreffen mit den Deutschen, besonders, wenn Transporte abgingen und die Abfahrenden nicht schnell genug einstiegen. Gewisse Vergehen, wie Besitz von Rauchwaren oder Geld (beides streng verboten) hatte Verschickung auf die kleine Festung, die den Deutschen unterstand, zur Folge und bedeutete meist Verschwinden für immer. Zu der psychischen Misshandlung gehörte die immerwährende Unruhe, in der wir gehalten wurden: Alle Befehle und Aufrufe kamen nachts, das Licht musste manchmal nachts für 1 Stunde eingeschaltet werden, Grund unbekannt: Besuche von Kontrollkommissionen wurden angesetzt, was eine geradezu ungeheuerliche Arbeitsbelastung in den Häusern bedeutete (Putzen, Aufräumen, Fegen usw.), die Kommission kam aber fast nie; Luftalarm zu den ausgefallensten Zeiten, ohne dass Flugzeuge in Sicht waren und die einen stundenlang in fremden Hausfluren zurückhielten, meistens zur Essensabholzeit. Das ständige Umziehen von einem Zimmer, von einem Haus, von einer Kaserne zur anderen, meist innerhalb einer oder weniger

a slice of sausage or a small piece of meat (often not fresh), alternatively a small portion of noodles, barley, or a small yeast dumpling with sauce in place of the potato, or a small flour dumpling. In the evening, 0.4 liters of soup, slightly thicker than at lunchtime. Also, one kilogram of bread to last three days. This also had to suffice for two dinners since twice for dinner there was only coffee. As a weekly ration we received sixty grams of butter, margarine, or some spicy spread. Never eggs, fish, butter, cheese, fruit, vegetables, etc. Vegetables we had a few times in the months before liberation. The results of this kind of nutrition were bone softening and hunger edemas, which often caused the death of those who were afflicted. When people fell, they usually suffered fractures, in most cases fractures of the neck of the femur. An example: Once I was given one hour to vacate my room in the hospital, where I was receiving treatment, because twenty-seven cases of that kind of fracture needed to be accommodated.

The way the Germans treated us cannot be compared with what they did in Auschwitz, Buchenwald, or similar concentration camps. We prisoners had no interactions with the Germans in our daily lives, but only privately and at work under Jewish supervision (Jewish ghetto police, ghetto court for theft, disobedience, etc., labor court, house and room eldest overseeing cleanliness, order, and discipline in the houses). A slap in the face, a blow with a cane, and other punishments were, of course, common when we occasionally encountered Germans, especially when transports were leaving, or prisoners did not get on the transport quickly enough. Certain infractions, such as the possession of tobacco products or money (both strictly prohibited) were punished by imprisonment in the "Small Fortress," which was under the control of the Germans, and usually meant disappearing forever. Part of the psychological abuse we were subjected to was keeping us in perpetual turmoil and trepidation: all orders and proclamations came at night, sometimes the lights had to be turned on for an hour in the middle of the night, for no apparent reason: Inspections by the control commission were announced but the commission almost never came. This led to a positively inordinate amount of work that had to be performed in the houses (cleaning, tidying up, sweeping, etc.); the air-raid siren went off at the most unusual times, with no planes in sight, and this kept us stuck for hours in others' houses, most of the time coinciding with mealtimes. The constant moving from one room, from one house, from one barracks to another always had to happen under intense time pressure and led to innumerable hassles and costs (we had to give bread and other groceries to the men who helped carry our possessions).

Stunden, das mit unzähligen Scherereien und Kosten verbunden war (man musste den Männern, die einem bei der Gepäckbeförderung halfen, Brot oder andere Lebensmittel geben). Ich selbst zog 17 mal dort um. Im Sommer 43 z. B. musste die Sudetenkaserne, in der 5 000 Männer wohnten, innerhalb von 58 Stunden geräumt werden und die Insassen wurden in andere bereits überfüllte Kasernen gestopft. Die Lagerstätten standen meistens so dicht beieinander, dass es unmöglich war, einen Durchgang offen zu halten, was natürlich höchst unhygienisch war. Zum Punkt Hygiene: Unser Brot wurde uns in Leichenwagen zugefahren und auf unsauberste Weise ins Haus getragen. Tod und Sterben bildete ein Kapitel für sich. Vorzügliche Ärzte, Kapazitäten aus Berlin, Wien und Prag betreuten die Kranken, die auch ihre eigene Diät erhielten, sogar Medikamente waren lange Zeit noch vorhanden, gingen aber im letzten Jahr vollkommen aus. Trotz der hochstehenden ärztlichen Versorgung wurden Tausende durch Entbehrung und Seuchen dahingerafft, und die Sterblichkeitsziffer war enorm, an manchen Tagen bis zu 150 Fällen, als Regel 30–50. Alle Toten wurden eingeäschert. Es fanden immer gemeinschaftliche Leichenfeiern für alle am selben Tag zu Bestattenden statt. Zu den Einäscherungen war niemand zugelassen. Es sei hier gleich erwähnt, dass kurze Zeit von der Befreiung, von deren Bevorstehen wir nichts wussten, alle Urnen auf Lastkraftwagen verladen und in die Elbe geworfen wurden, damit nicht mehr festzustellen sei, wie viel Tausende dort zugrunde gegangen waren. Auch das gesamte Registrationsmaterial von allen Ämtern wurde vor Abmarsch der Deutschen restlos vernichtet, tagelang brannten Scheiterhaufen und Öfen, und die Stadt war in einen Aschenregen gehüllt, so dass es vollkommen unmöglich ist, festzustellen, wer je in Th. gewesen ist. Das Gleiche soll auch in allen anderen Konzentrationslagern der Fall gewesen sein.–

Wenn eine ausländische Kommission angesagt war, wurden Potemkinsche Dörfer aufgestellt, d. h. es gab erhöhte Essensrationen, aus Prag kamen allerlei schöne Dinge, die verteilt wurden, die Einwohner mussten gut gekleidet durch die Straßen promenieren, wer nichts anständiges anzuziehen hatte, musste daheim bleiben, und die Kinder spielten fröhlich auf den Spielplätzen, die zu diesem Zweck hergerichtet waren. Die Auslagen der Geschäfte waren wunderschön ausgestattet, aber nichts von den zur Schau gestellten Waren war verkäuflich. Zum Glück merkten manche der ausländischen Delegierten, wie die Zustände wirklich waren. Unnötig zu bemerken, dass keiner von ihnen je die Elendsquartiere sah, sondern nur einige eigens hergerichtete Renommierräume. Ein Propagandafilm für

I myself moved seventeen times while at Theresienstadt. For example, in the summer of '43 the "Sudeten Barracks," which housed 5,000 men, had to be vacated within a period of fifty-eight hours, and the inmates were crammed into another, already overcrowded barracks. The beds were lined up so close to each other that it was impossible to walk between them, which was highly insanitary of course. About hygiene: our bread was brought to us on hearses and carried into the houses in a most unhygienic way. Death and dying was a chapter in itself. Excellent doctors, well-known experts from Berlin, Vienna, and Prague cared for the ill who received a special diet, even medication was available for quite a while; in the last year there was none, however. Despite the outstanding medical care, thousands fell victim to destitution and infectious diseases, and the mortality rate was enormous, some days up to 150, on average 30–50. All the dead were cremated. Collective funeral rites took place every day for all who had died. No one was admitted to the cremations. I would like to mention at this point that all urns were loaded onto lorries and tossed into the Elbe River shortly before we were liberated, which was a moment that we did not anticipate. This was done to destroy evidence of how many thousands had perished here. Also, all registration papers and materials from all offices were destroyed before the Germans left, for days fires were burning outside and in furnaces, and the whole town was wrapped in a cloud of ash. The fallout is that it will never ever be possible to determine the identities of everyone who had ever been in Th. The same is said to have been done in all other concentration camps too.

Whenever a foreign commission was scheduled to come to Th., Potemkin villages were erected, i.e. food rations were increased, all kinds of beautiful things were brought in from Prague and distributed to us, the inhabitants were required to dress nicely and promenade on the streets. Those who did not own any presentable clothing had to stay inside, the children played merrily in the playgrounds that were prettified for this occasion. The shop windows were filled with ample goods, beautifully displayed, but none of the showcased goods were for sale. Fortunately, some of the foreign delegates realized what conditions were actually like. Needless to say, none of them ever saw the squalid quarters we lived in, but instead only a few specially prepared showrooms. A propaganda film for neutral countries, entitled *The Führer Gives a City to the Jews*, was made in the same manner: While none of us ever laid eyes on a river there (we were not allowed to leave the ghetto), they created a pool by the Elbe River, outside of the town, and showed people frolicking in the water, swimsuits and beachwear were brought in from

neutrale Länder „Hitler schenkt den Juden eine Stadt" wurde im gleichen Genre gedreht: Während keiner von uns je einen Fluss dort sah (wir durften das Ghetto nicht verlassen) wurde an der Elbe ausserhalb der Stadt eine Badeanstalt mit lustigem Badebetrieb arrangiert, Bade- und Strandanzüge kamen aus Prag. Tanzbetrieb im Cafe oder im Freien, riesige Geschäftigkeit auf der Post, wo Berge von Paketen ausgeliefert wurden und Briefe verteilt, wenn in Wirklichkeit zahllose Pakete von den Nazis gestohlen wurden, bei jedem ankommenden Paket in Gegenwart des Empfängers eine genaue Kontrolle stattfand und ein Teil des Inhalts als Contrebande herausgenommen wurde. Man durfte offiziell einmal im Monat, zuletzt alle 2 Monate eine Postkarte mit 30 Worten schreiben, je nach Laune der Kommandanten wurde die ganze einlaufende oder abzusendende Post in den Ofen geworfen.

Erwähnt seien noch die sog. Kontrollen nach Geld und Cigaretten, bei denen die Einwohner ihr Zimmer zu verlassen hatten, von 4 Leuten alles genau untersucht wurde und alles, was ihnen gefiel, mit fortgenommen wurde. Es gab für Th. eigens gedrucktes Geld, auf dem Moses mit den Gesetzestafeln abgebildet war. Damit wurde ein Teil der Gehälter ausgezahlt, und man konnte periodisch kleine Einkäufe machen, z. B. Senf, Selleriesalz, Teesurrogat, doch niemals Brot oder richtige Nahrungsmittel, auch Wäsche und Kleider—alles aus den gestohlenen Koffern. Den aus Deutschland nach Th. deportierten Juden wurde das Gepäck überhaupt nicht ausgeliefert. Dass bei dieser Art von Leben alle schlechten Eigenschaften des Menschen zum Vorschein kamen, besonders jede Art von Diebstahl, hauptsächlich von Nahrungsmitteln an der Tagesordnung war, ist begreiflich. Auch Kinder wurden zum Stehlen abgerichtet, und beneidet wurden die Eltern, deren Buben besonders geschickt im „Schleusen" von Kartoffeln waren. Der Schrecklichste der Schrecken waren die nach Polen abgehenden Transporte, die Alte und Junge, Kranke und Gesunde, Inhaber der höchsten Stellen wie auch Arbeitsunfähige umfassten. Die Aufrufe erfolgten mitten in der Nacht, die Aufgerufenen mussten mit wenig Gepäck sofort in die Schleuse und durften nicht mehr heraus, auf abgesperrten Strassen wurden sie von Gendarmerie zum Bahnhof gebracht und meist in Güterwagen zusammengepfercht wie die Heringe verladen. Verschiedentlich kam es vor, dass das spärliche Gepäck auf dem Bahnhof stehen blieb, wenn der Kommandant das Abfahrzeichen zu früh gab, natürlich absichtlich. Solche Transporte umfassten 1200–1500 Menschen, die Herbsttransporte im Jahre 44 beförderten 15–20 000 Menschen nach Polen, darunter viele in sterbendem Zustand. Die Transporte gingen als sog. Arbeitstransporte mit dem Reiseziel

Prague. There was dancing in the café or outdoors, bustling activity at the post office where they showed mountains of packages and letters being processed for delivery. Yet in reality the Nazis stole countless packages, inspected every incoming package in the presence of the addressee, and confiscated part of the contents as contraband. Officially, we were allowed to write one postcard per month, later only every two months, consisting of thirty words, and every now and then the commandant decided on a whim that all mail, incoming and outgoing, would be tossed into a furnace.

I should also mention the so-called money and cigarette controls. When these occurred, the residents had to leave their rooms, four inspectors searched through everything meticulously, and if they liked anything, they simply took it with them. There was money, printed specially for Th., and it showed Moses and the Tablets of the Law. With this currency, part of the wages was paid out, and we could occasionally make small purchases, as for example mustard, celery salt, tea substitute, but never bread or actually nutritious food, also underwear and clothes—all of it came from stolen suitcases. The Jews who had been deported from Germany to Th. never received their luggage at all. It is understandable that the bad traits of humanity regularly came to the fore in this kind of environment, especially all kinds of thievery. People stole mainly food, and even children were trained to steal. Those parents whose boys were adept at "redirecting" potatoes were viewed with envy. The worst of all horrors were the transports leaving for Poland, usually consisting of all different kinds of people, old and young, sick and healthy, holders of the most important positions and people unable to work. The summons came in the middle of the night, those who were called had to go to "The Sluice" and could not come out again. They were not allowed to take much with them, they were driven down sealed-off streets by the gendarmes, and then at the train station loaded onto freight cars, packed tightly like herrings. On various occasions, some of their meager possessions were left behind at the train station when the commandant ordered the train to depart too soon, which was intentional of course. These kinds of transports carried 1,200–1,500 people; the transports in the fall of 1944 moved 15–20,000 people to Poland, many of them already dying. The transports departed as so-called labor transports headed to Germany; fortunately, neither the people departing nor the ones staying behind knew the truth: that the transports were actually headed to Auschwitz and the people in them, in most instances, to the gas chambers. We were astonished when we noticed that transports from various Polish and German camps were coming back to Th. in March 1945.

Deutschland weg; dass sie tatsächlich alle nach Auschwitz und grösstenteils in die Gaskammern wanderten, wussten zum Glück weder die Abreisenden noch die Zurückbleibenden. Zum allgemeinen Erstaunen kamen im März 45 einige Transporte aus den verschiedensten polnischen und deutschen Lagern nach Th. zurück, allerdings in unbeschreiblichem Zustand, wie lebende Leichname durch die Straßen wankend, zum Teil so schwach, dass sie auf Bahren herausbefördert werden mussten und zum grossen Teil starben. Ein ganzer Waggon voll Leichen kam mit an und im Duschraum des Zentralbades, wo die Menschen gesäubert werden sollten, fielen 25 bei der Berührung mit dem heissen Wasser aus Schwäche tot um. Sie hatten alle kaum mehr etwas Menschliches an sich und glichen wilden Tieren.

Als Lichtblick möchte ich die Organisation „Freizeitgestaltung" erwähnen. Sie sorgte für Darbietung ausgezeichneter musikalischer Genüsse, besass ein eigenes Orchester, geleitet von bekannten Dirigenten und Solisten allerersten Ranges, die durch Opern, Oratorien und prachtvolle Konzerte hohe Genüsse boten. Vorträge auf allen Gebieten menschlichen Wissens von Gelehrten gehalten, boten Anregung und Belehrung.

Das furchtbarste Erlebnis während unsers Dortseins war der Tag der „Volkszählung" in Bauschowitz am 9. November 1943, wo die damals 35 000 jüdische Menschen umfassende Bevölkerung von Th. in der Morgenfrühe in einen mächtigen Talkessel, eine Stunde von der Stadt entfernt, geführt wurde. Nur die gehunfähigen Kranken wurden in der vorhergehenden Nacht in die Krankenhäuser gebracht, während Greise ebenso wie Säuglinge 12–14 Stunden den kalten Novembertrag draußen verbrachten und von dem kleinen Mundvorrat zehrend (ohne einen warmen Bissen oder einen Tropfen Wasser) des Schicksals harrten, das ihnen bestimmt war. Diese Ungewissheit verbunden mit der furchtbaren körperlichen Anstrengung des Stehens (keinerlei Sitzgelegenheit war vorhanden) liess viele zusammenbrechen. Bewusstlos daliegende Alte, vor Hunger laut weinende Kinder, verzweifelte Männer und Frauen ringsum, bis in finsterer Nacht der Befehl zur Rückkehr ins Ghetto als Erlösungsruf ertönte. Die Volkszählung, als solche von den Deutschen scheinbar vorgenommen, war eine Farce, denn jeder Einwohner war mindestens 10mal registriert. Keiner, der diesen Tag miterlebte, wird ihn jemals vergessen.

The people who emerged, however, were in an indescribable condition, staggering around like the living dead, many of them so weakened that they had to be carried on stretchers and died soon thereafter. One time, a whole train car filled with corpses arrived. In the showers of the main bathhouse, where the people from the transports were to be washed, twenty-five of them were so frail that they fell down and died on the spot when they came into contact with hot water. There was no longer anything human about them, and they resembled wild animals.

As a bright spot, I would like to mention the "Office for Leisure-Time Activities." It organized performances of outstanding musical quality, had its own orchestra, led by a well-known conductor and soloists of the highest rank, who regaled us with magnificent operas, oratorios, and concerts. In addition, there were presentations from all areas of human knowledge and inquiry, given by scholars. These talks offered intellectual stimulation and edification.

The worst experience during our confinement was the day of the "census" in Bauschowitz on November 9, 1943. In the early morning of that day, the entire population of Th., which amounted to 35,000 Jews at that time, was taken to a gigantic basin, about one hour away from the town. Those who were unable to walk were taken to the hospitals during the previous night, but old men just the same as infants had to spend twelve to fourteen hours outside, on this cold November day, with little to eat (nothing warm and not a drop of water), waiting to meet the fate that had been determined for them. This uncertainty, combined with the terrible physical exertion that resulted from standing upright (there was no place to sit anywhere), caused many to collapse. Old people were lying on the ground unconscious, starving children were crying, desperate men and women all around, until, to great relief, the order to return to the ghetto was finally given at nightfall. The census the Germans claimed to be conducting was a farce, since every inhabitant had been registered and recorded at least ten times already. No one who lived through that day will ever forget it.

Die Kristallnacht
(9. bis 10. November 1938)

Rede des Dr. Goebbels an die auslaendische Presse am 10. November:

‚Alle herumschwirrenden Geruechte ueber Gewalttaten gegen Juden im ganzen Reich sind frei erfunden. Keinem Juden in ganz Deutschland ist ein Haar gekruemmt worden, juedisches Eigentum wurde weder beschaedigt, noch vernichtet. Wenn es je zu unbedeutenden Zwischenfaellen kam, so hat sich eben die entruestete Bevoelkerung über den Tod von Herrn vom Rath Luft gemacht.'

Hier die einwandfrei festgestellte Illustration zu diesen Ausfuehrungen:

In der Streicher-Stadt Nuernberg, wo es bekanntlich zu den schlimmsten Ausschreitungen kam, war die SA frueh um ½ 2 auf dem Hauptmarkt versammelt, bekam Stahlruten und Schlaginstrumente ueberreicht und dazu genau Anweisungen ueber die vorzunehmenden Verwuestungen und Zerstoerungen aller juedischen Wohnungen, ebenso wie man die Juden misshandeln solle; Parole des Gauleiters: ‚Auf eine Handvoll Juden mehr oder weniger kommt es nicht an!' Streicher erklaerte bekanntlich in seiner Verteidigung vor dem Nuernberger Tribunal, dass er niemals zu Gewalttaten gegen Juden aufgehetzt hat. Eine Anzahl von Juden wurden durch's Fenster oder die Treppe hinuntergeworfen, und blieben tot liegen, zahllose kamen schwerverwundet mit gebrochenen Gliedern und furchtbaren Quetschungen und Schlagwunden ins juedische Krankenhaus der Nachbarstadt Fuerth; Selbstmorde ereigneten sich in grosser Zahl.

Szenen beim Vernichten juedischer Wohnungen: alle Gemaelde wurden zerschnitten. Ein Kunstsammler, Besitzer einer Rembrandtskizze, bot dieses Meisterwerk der eindringenden SA mit den Worten an: ‚Zerstoeren Sie dies einzigartige Werk nicht, nehmen Sie es mit, es ist unersetzlich!' Die Antwort war ein vollstaendiges Zerschnitzeln dieser Skizze. Eine weinende Frau bat: ‚Koennen Sie nicht wenigstens das Oelbild meines verstorbenen Vaters verschonen?' ‚Gehen Sie hinaus, wenn Sie nicht zuschauen wollen', lautete die Entgegnung, als die Messer in das Bild fuhren. Und der Mutter eines im Weltkrieg gefallenen Sohnes, die sein Bild im Arm hielt und es unter Traenen verteidigt, wurde es entrissen und mit genagelten Stiefeln zertrampelt.

The Night of Broken Glass
(November 9–10, 1938)

Speech by Dr. Goebbels to the foreign press on November 10:

"All the rumors that are flying around about violent acts against Jews in the whole Reich are pure fabrications. No Jew in all of Germany has been harmed in the least, Jewish property has neither been damaged nor destroyed. If any minor incidents did in fact occur, this happened because the people were venting their anger about the death of Herr vom Rath."

Here follows the well-documented illustration of these remarks:

In Nuremberg, the city of Streicher, where, as is well known, some of the worst rioting occurred, the *SA* gathered at 1:30 at night on the *Hauptmarkt*. They received steel pipes and other batons as well as detailed instructions for carrying out the planned vandalization and destruction of all Jewish residences, and for how to abuse the Jews; the *Gauleiter's* rallying cry: "A handful of Jews more or less, it doesn't matter!" As is well known, Streicher stated in his defense at the Nuremberg trials that he never incited violence against the Jews. Some Jews were thrown out the window or pushed down a stairwell and left for dead, many others arrived at the Jewish hospital in the neighboring city of Fürth with serious injuries, with broken limbs, terrible bruises, and wounds from the beatings. Suicides occurred in great numbers.

Scenes from the destruction of Jewish residences: all paintings were cut into pieces. An art collector, owner of a Rembrandt sketch, offered this masterpiece to the *SA* men who were barging in: "Do not destroy this unique work, take it with you, it is irreplaceable!" They responded by completely shredding this sketch. A wailing woman pleaded: "Couldn't you at least spare the oil painting of my deceased father?" They countered with "Leave if you don't want to watch," as they drove a knife into the painting. The mother of a man who died in World War I held a picture of him in her arms and shielded it, in tears. They tore it away from her and trampled on it with their jackboots.

An *SA* unit broke into a newly constructed villa, which was surrounded by beautiful gardens. The owner recognized in the leader of the horde the landscape architect who had been paid handsomely for designing her gardens; when she pointed this out to him he replied: "And now I'll just demolish it!"

Ein Trupp SA drang in eine neuerbaute Villa, die von einem schoenen Park umgeben war. Im Anfuehrer der Horde erkannte die Besitzerin den Gartenarchitekten, der fuer Tausende von Mark den Garten angelegt hatte; ihren Hinweis darauf beantwortete er: ‚Und jetzt zerstoere ich ihn wieder!'—Die orthodoxe Synagoge wurde niedergebrannt (die liberale war schon im Sommer '38 auf Befehl Streichers vollständig zerstoert und abgerissen worden!) die Truemmer, die die Strasse bedeckten, wurden entfernt, die Rechnung dafuer musste die Gemeinde bezahlen. In Fuerth hatte die Schuljugend die Grabsteine auf dem juedischen Friedhof systematisch umgeworfen; ein Kind verletzte sich dabei und musste sich in aerztliche Behandlung begeben, die Doktorsrechnung wurde der Kultusgemeinde vorgelegt.—Bemerkung eines Fuerther Feuerwehrmannes vor der brennenden Synagoge: ‚27 Jahre lange habe ich Braende geloescht, es ist das erste Mal, dass ich heute einen anlegen musste!' Eine bekannte juedische Persoenlichkeit sollte verhaftet werden, da der Betreffende geschaeftlich verreist war, wollte man an seiner Stelle seine Frau und sein krankes Kind mitnehmen. Die Frau wies auf das in hohem Fieber liegende Kind, es könne in dieser kalten Novembernacht bei einem Abtransport ernstlichen Schaden erleiden, Antwort: ‚Umso besser, dann krepiert es eher!' Unnoetig zu sagen, dass auch viele Kinder mit Kopfwunden und Misshandlungen ins juedische Krankenhaus eingeliefert wurden. In diesem Krankenhaus lagen etliche frisch operierte Kranke; sie mussten vor den hereinstroemenden SA-Scharen stramm stehen, Folge: Todesfaelle an Embolie und Verblutung.

Das sind einige kleine Ausschnitte, sie koennten durch hunderte ergaenzt werden.

In unserer raschlebigen Zeit wird nur allzurasch vergessen, so auch die Episoden jener Tage, die die Einstellung des Grossteils der deutschen Bevoelkerung widerspiegeln. Man hat so grosses Mitleid mit ihr, der unschuldigen Bevoelkerung, die ja bekanntlich ‚von nichts wusste', aber hier aktiv und passiv die Ereignisse miterlebte. Daran soll wieder einmal erinnert werden.

E.D.

The Orthodox synagogue was burnt down (the Liberal one had already been completely destroyed and demolished in the summer of 1938 on the orders of Streicher!), the debris that had fallen onto the street was removed, and the congregation had to foot the bill. In Fürth, students had systematically toppled the tombstones in the Jewish cemetery. One of the children was hurt during this action and had to be treated by a doctor, the bill was later presented to the congregation. Remarks made by a Fürth fireman in front of the burning synagogue: "For twenty-seven years I have been extinguishing fires, today was the first time that I've had to start a fire." A well-known Jewish individual was to be arrested but since he was away on a business trip they wanted to take his wife and ailing child instead. The woman pointed out that the child, who had a fever, could be seriously harmed if transported through the city in this cold November night. The answer: "All the better, then it will croak sooner!" Needless to say, there were also many children admitted to the Jewish hospital, suffering from head wounds and other abuses. In this hospital, there were many recently operated patients; they had to stand at attention for the SA squads that came marching in. The result: Fatalities due to embolisms and exsanguinations.

These are but brief glimpses, I could add hundreds more.

In our fast-moving times we tend to forget all too quickly. Take for example the events of those days, which reflected the mindset of a large portion of the German populace. There is so much pity for them now, those innocent Germans who, as everyone knows, "knew nothing about anything going on." Here, they were involved both actively and passively. Let's remember that.

E.D.

Bibliography

Primary Literature

Works by Else Dormitzer

Theresienstädter Bilder. Hilversum: De Boekenvriend, 1945.

Berühmte Jüdische Frauen in Vergangenheit und Gegenwart. Berlin: Philo, 1925.

Jubiläumsschrift zum 25jährigen Bestehen des Nürnberger Feuerbestattungs-Vereins 1891–1916. Nürnberg: ca. 1916.

Kulturträger der Gegenwart über die Feuerbestattung. Interviews conducted by Else Dormitzer-Dorn on assignment of the German-Language Union for Fire Burials. Nuremberg: Thümmel, 1913.

Selection of essays and articles

In books

"Judentum und Feuerbestattung." In *Religion und Feuerbestattung*, edited by Nürnberger Feuerbestattungsverein, 12–15. Nuremberg: Wilh. Tümmels Buchdruckerei, 1912.

In newspapers and magazines

"Momentbilder des häuslichen Lebens." *Fränkischer Kurier,* December 28, 1906.

"Die Welt der Frau: Das Gästebuch." *Generalanzeiger Frankfurt am Main,* November 16, 1907.

"Kulinarisch." *Generalanzeiger Frankfurt am Main,* October 2, 1908.

"Ein Besuch im Säuglingsheim." *Werde gesund,* May 1, 1908.

"Nürnberger Theaterbrief." *Coburger Tageblatt,* May 12, 1908.

"Liesels Heiratspläne." *Zeitschrift für Kinderpflege,* December 1908.

"Frühlingsfahrt durch die Fränkische Schweiz." *Fränkischer Kurier,* May 30, 1909.

"Bayrische Steuerpanik. Ein Stimmungsbild aus der letzten Oktoberwoche." *Zweites Morgenblatt der Frankfurter Zeitung,* November 2, 1911.

"Die jüdische Frau in der Propaganda." *Liberales Judentum* 5–6 (1917): 66–68.

"Erfahrungen aus meiner Werbetätigkeit." *Im deutschen Reich* 3 (1917): 121–123.

"Die Forderung der jüdischen Frau." *Liberales Judentum* 3–4 (1919): 26–28.

"Die Frau und der Centralverein." *CV-Zeitung* 1 (1922): 7–8.

"Ein Freitagabend in der Hauptsynagoge zu Rom." *Nürnberger Israelitisches Gemeindeblatt* 5, no. 11–12 (1925): 92–93.

"Auf den Spuren des Rabbi Löw." *Jüdisch-Liberale Zeitung* 25 (1928): 3.

"Paul Nathan. Ein Lebensbild von Ernst Feder." *Nürnberger-Fürther Israelitisches Gemeindeblatt* 9, no. 5 (1929): 91–92.

"Dem Redaktionskollegen des Nürnberger-Fürther Gemeindeblatts." *Nürnberger-Fürther Israelitisches Gemeindeblatt* 11, no. 1 (1933): 111.

"Männer der Feder sprechen." *Nürnberger-Fürther Israelitisches Gemeindeblatt* 13, no. 1 (1933): 3.

"Die Kameradin des Mannes." Beilage *Jüdisch-Liberale Zeitung* no. 4 (1933).

"Bauschowitz." *The Synagogue Review*, December 1946, 53–54.

"Children in Theresienstadt." *Association of Jewish Refugees Information*, May 1947.

"High Holidays—Then and Now." *Our Congregation*, September/October 1947.

"Remembrance of Terezin." *Association of Jewish Refugees Information*, May 1948.

"Erinnerungen an Theresienstadt." *Filantropia* [Buenos Aires], June 1948.

"Memories of November 10, 1938." *The Synagogue Review*, November 1948.

"Remember Amalek: Thoughts after Purim." *The Synagogue Review*, April 1949.

"The Jewish Woman." *The Synagogue Review*, February 1950, 133.

"Theresienstadt Five Years Ago." *Association of Jewish Refugees Information*, May 1950.

"Rotary in a Concentration Camp." *The Rotarian*, 1952.

Testimonial Reports

"Erlebnisse in Nürnberg, Holland, Theresienstadt und beim Rücktransport nach Holland."

"Leben in Theresienstadt."

"Die Kristallnacht."

Works by Else Dorn (pseudonym)

Geburtstagsfreuden von kleinen Leuten. 1935. No further information.

Auf dem Hühnerhof. Nuremberg: Verlag Gebrüder Bing, 1930.

Allerlei Zeitvertreib. Berlin: Pestalozzi-Verlags Anstalt, 1927.

Am Meeresstrand. Berlin: Pestalozzi Verlags-Anstalt, 1927.

Ferien an der See. Berlin: Pestalozzi Verlags-Anstalt, 1927.

Gute Freunde vom Lande. Berlin: Pestalozzi Verlags-Anstalt, 1927.

Gute Kameraden. Berlin: Pestalozzi Verlags-Anstalt, 1927.

Hurra, Hurra, jetzt sind wir da. Berlin: Pestalozzi Verlags-Anstalt, 1927.

Kinderfreuden. Berlin: Pestalozzi Verlags-Anstalt, 1927.

Komische Tiere. Berlin: Pestalozzi Verlags-Anstalt, 1927.

Ländliche Freuden. Berlin: Pestalozzi Verlags-Anstalt, 1927.

Lasst's euch schmecken. Berlin: Pestalozzi Verlags-Anstalt, 1927.

Lustiges vom Land. Berlin: Pestalozzi Verlags-Anstalt, 1927.

Was spielen wir? Berlin: Pestalozzi Verlags-Anstalt, 1927.

Wilde und zahme Tiere. Berlin: Pestalozzi Verlags-Anstalt, 1927.

Auf zur Weltreise. Fürth: Löwensohn, 1925.

Das Zauberpferd. Zurich: Ernst Waldmann, 1925.

Dem braven Kind vom Osterhas. 1925. No further information.

Klein Dorchen und ihr Mohrchen. 1925. No further information.

Rings um die Erde geht der Ritt, Ihr lieben Kleinen kommet mit! Fürth: Löwensohn, 1925.

Allerlei Tiere. Nuremberg: Bing Verlag, ca. 1922.

Schnick, Schnack, Schnucki und die Waldhexe. 1921. No further information.

Was das Kind erfreut. 1920. No further information.

Wie fleißige Kinder die Zeit sich vertreiben Mit Kochen und Waschen, mit Lesen und Schreiben. 1900. No further information.

Unsere Muh-Kuh. Nuremberg: Verlag Gebrüder Bing. No further information.

Von zehn kleinen Kinderlein soll euch heut erzählet sein! No further information.

Schnick-Schnack-Schnucki. No further information.

Translations into German

Shakespeare-Erzählungen nach Lamb. Fürth: Löwensohn, 1913.

Des Pilzlingsvolkes lustiges Treiben Will ich in Bild und Wort beschreiben. 1910. No further information.

Fairy Tales and Stories

"Traumland." In *Für die Dämmerstunde. Neue Märchen und Geschichten*, edited by Elisabeth Dauthendey, 46–50. Fürth: Löwensohn, 1928.

"Die Zauberfeder." In *Für die Dämmerstunde. Neue Märchen und Geschichten*, edited by Elisabeth Dauthendey, 18–20. Fürth: Löwensohn, 1928.

"Wie Hänschen wieder gesund wurde." In *Für die Dämmerstunde. Neue Märchen und Geschichten*, edited by Elisabeth Dauthendey, 70–73. Fürth: Löwensohn, 1928.

"Was sich die Weihnachtsbäume erzählen." In *Für die Dämmerstunde. Neue Märchen und Geschichten*, edited by Elisabeth Dauthendey, 119–124. Fürth: Löwensohn, 1928.

"Der Englein Tageslauf." In *Das neue Frida Schanz Buch, Jubiläumsband. Neue Märchen, Erzählungen, Gedichte*, edited by Walter Günther Schreckenbach, 71–73. Fürth: Löwensohn, 1929.

"Das Kräutlein 'Tu dich um.'" In *Das neue Frida Schanz Buch, Jubiläumsband. Neue Märchen, Erzählungen, Gedichte*, edited by Walter Günther Schreckenbach, 112–115. Fürth: Löwensohn, 1929.

Secondary Literature

Aaron, Frieda W. *Bearing the Unbearable: Yiddish and Polish Poetry in the Ghettos and Concentration Camps*. Albany: SUNY Press, 1990.

Adler, H. G. *Theresienstadt 1941–1945. Das Antlitz einer Zwangsgemeinschaft*. Tübingen: Mohr, 1955.

Adorno, Theodor W. "Kulturkritik und Gesellschaft." In idem, *Gesammelte Schriften*, volume 10, part 1, edited by Rolf Tiedemann, 409–506. Frankfurt: Suhrkamp, 1996.

Alfers, Sandra. *weiter schreiben. Leben und Lyrik der Else Dormitzer*. Berlin: Hentrich & Hentrich, 2015.

———. "Else Dormitzer's *Theresienstädter Bilder*: Poetry, Testimony, and the Holocaust." *Études Arméniennes Contemporaines* 3, no. 5 (2015): *Special Edition: Victim Testimony and Understanding Mass Violence*, edited by Alexandra Garbarini and Boris Adjemian, 139–159.

———. "'Writing From Within': Else Dormitzer in Theresienstadt, 1943–45." *Journal of Teaching and Education* 1, no. 4 (2012): 141–147.

———. "The Precariousness of Genre: German-Language Poetry from the Holocaust." *Oxford German Studies* 39, no. 3 (2010): 271–289.

———. "Poetry from the Theresienstadt Transit Camp." *Rocky Mountain Review* 61, no. 1 (2010): 47–70.

———. "Voices from a Haunting Past: Ghosts, Memory, and Poetry in Ruth Klüger's *weiter leben. Eine Jugend* (1992)." *Monatshefte* 100, no. 4 (2008): 1–15.

———. "Metaphern der Auflösung: Der Tod als poetische Grenzerfahrung in 'Das Sterben' von Gertrud Kantorowicz (1876–1945)." In *Theresienstädter Studien und Dokumente*, edited by Jaroslava Milotová, Anna Hájková, and Michael Wögerbauer, 150–161. Prague: Sefer, 2006.

———. "Vergessene Verse: Untersuchungen zur deutschsprachigen Lyrik aus Theresienstadt." In *Theresienstädter Studien und Dokumente*, edited by Jaroslava Milotová, Ulf Rathgeber, and Michael Wögerbauer, 137–158. Prague: Sefer, 2004.

———. "Wohin schwankt ihr noch eh' der Atem schwand? Untersuchungen zur deutschsprachigen Lyrik aus Theresienstadt (1941–1945)." PhD diss., University of Massachusetts, Amherst, 2003.

Arnold, Heinz Ludwig, ed. *Text und Kritik. Zeitschrift für Literatur* 163 (July 2004): *H. G. Adler*.

Auburger, Thomas. "Die Staatspolizeistelle Nürnberg-Fürth." In *Entrechtet. Entwürdigt. Beraubt. Die Arisierung in Nürnberg und Fürth*, edited by Matthias Henkel and Eckart Dietzelfelbinger, 113–121. Petersberg: Michael Imhof, 2012.

Ausländer, Rose. *Gesammelte Werke*. Volume 3: *Hügel, aus Äther, unwiderruflich. Gedichte und Prosa 1966–1975*. Edited by Helmut Braun. Frankfurt: S. Fischer, 1984.

Barkai, Avraham. *"Wehr Dich!" Der Centralverein deutscher Staatsbürger jüdischen Glaubens 1893–1938*. Munich: C. H. Beck, 2002.

Barut, Yaakov. "Jüdisches Leben in Franken während des Nationalsozialismus." In *Die Juden in Franken*, edited by Michael Brenner and Daniela F. Eisenstein, 219–250. Munich: Oldenbourg, 2012.

Baumann, Ulrich, and François Guesnet. "Kristallnacht-Pogrom-State Terror: A Terminological Reflection." In *New Perspectives on Kristallnacht: After 80 Years, the Nazi Pogrom in Global Comparison*, edited by Steven J. Ross, Wolf Gruner, and Lisa Ansell, 1–15. West Lafayette: Indiana University Press, 2019.

Benz, Wolfgang. *Theresienstadt. Eine Geschichte von Täuschung und Vernichtung*. Munich: C. H. Beck, 2013.

Beckermann, Michael. "Postcard from New York-Trio from Terezín." *Music & Politics* 1, no. 1 (2007): 1–19.

Berenbaum, Michael. "Foreword." In *In Memory's Kitchen: A Legacy from the Women of Theresienstadt*, edited by Cara de Silva, translated by Bianca Steiner Brown, ix–xvi. Northvale: J. Aronson, 1996.

———. *A Promise to Remember. The Holocaust in the Words and Voices of Its Survivors*. Boston: Bulfinch Press, 2003.

Berger-Dittscheid, Cornelia. "Zwischen Reform und Tradition—die Synagogen des 19. und 20. Jahrhunderts in Nürnberg." In *Geschichte und Kultur der Juden in Nürnberg*, edited by Andrea M. Kluxen and Julia Krieger, 213–245. Würzburg: Ergon, 2014.

Berghahn, Marion. *German-Jewish Refugees in England. The Ambiguities of Assimilation*. New York: St. Martin's Press, 1984.

Boas, Jacob. *Boulevard des Misères. The Story of Transit Camp Westerbork*. Hamden, CT: Archon Books, 1985.

Braun, Matthias Klaus. "Die Stadtverwaltung Nürnberg und ihre Beteiligung an der Arisierung." In *Entrechtet. Entwürdigt. Beraubt. Die Arisierung in Nürnberg und Fürth*, edited by Matthias Henkel and Eckart Dietzfelbinger, 123–137. Petersberg: Michael Imhof, 2012.

Brenner, Michael, and Daniela F. Eisenstein, eds. *Die Juden in Franken*. Munich: Oldenbourg, 2012.

Creet, Julia, Sara Horowitz, and Amira Bojadzija-Dan, eds. *H. G. Adler: Life, Literature, Legacy*. Evanston, IL: Northwestern University Press, 2016.

de Haan, Ido. "The Jewish Honor Court in the Netherlands." In *Jewish Honor Courts. Revenge, Retribution, and Reconciliation in Europe and Israel after the War*, edited by Laura Jokusch and Gabriel N. Finder, 107–136. Detroit: Wayne State University Press, 2015.

Denz, Rebekka. *Bürgerlich, Jüdisch, Weiblich. Die Frauen im Centralverein deutscher Staatsbürger Jüdischen Glaubens*. Berlin: Neofelis, 2021.

Dutlinger, Anne, ed. *Art, Music and Education as Strategies for Survival: Theresienstadt*. New York: Herodias, 2000.

Eichendorff, Joseph Freiherr von. *Eichendorff Gedichte*. Edited by Traude Dienel. Frankfurt: Suhrkamp, 1977. Accessed October 4, 2014. http://gutenberg.spiegel.de/buch/joseph-von-eichendorff-gedichte-4294/46.

Ekman, Stig, and Klas Åmark, eds. *Sweden's Relations with Nazism, Nazi Germany and the Holocaust*. Stockholm: Almqvist & Wiksell International, 2003.

Eke, Norbert Otto, and Hartmut Steineke, eds. *Shoah in der deutschsprachigen Literatur*. Berlin: Erich Schmidt, 2006.

Fischer, Saskia, Mareike Gronich, and Joanna Bednarska-Kociolek, eds. *Lagerliteratur. Schreibweisen, Zeugnisse, Didaktik*. Berlin: Peter Lang, 2021.

Gilbert, Sherli. *Music in the Holocaust: Confronting Life in the Nazi Ghettos and Camps*. Oxford: Oxford University Press, 2005.

Grenville, Anthony. *Continental Britons. Jewish Refugees from Nazi Europe*. London: The Association of Jewish Refugees and The Jewish Museum, 2021. Accessed April 28, 2022. https://ajr.org.uk/wp-content/uploads/2021/07/Continental-Britons-web-friendly-PDF.pdf.

Gruner, Wolf. *Die Judenverfolgung im Protektorat Böhmen und Mähren. Lokale Initiativen, Zentrale Entscheidungen, Jüdische Antworten 1939–1945*. Göttingen: Wallstein, 2016.

Hagen, Joshua, and Robert Ostergren. "Spectacle, Architecture and Place at the Nuremberg Party Rallies: Projecting a Nazi Vision of Past, Present and Future." *Cultural Geographies* 13, no. 2 (2006): 157–181.

Hájková, Anna. *The Last Ghetto. An Everyday History of Theresienstadt*. Oxford: Oxford University Press, 2020.

———. "Mutmaßungen über deutsche Juden: Alte Menschen aus Deutschland im Theresienstädter Ghetto." In *Alltag im Holocaust: Jüdisches Leben im Großdeutschen Reich 1941–1945*, edited by Andrea Löw, Doris L. Bergen, and Anna Hájková, 179–198. Munich: Oldenbourg, 2013.

Hambrecht, Rainer. *Die Braune Bastion. Der Aufstieg der NSDAP in Mittel- und Oberfranken (1922–1933)*. Petersberg: Michael Imhof, 2017.

Hecht, Cornelia. *Deutsche Juden und Antisemitismus in der Weimarer Republik*. Bonn: Dietz, 2003.

Henkel, Matthias, and Eckart Dietzfelbinger, eds. *Entrechtet. Entwürdigt. Beraubt. Die Arisierung in Nürnberg und Fürth*. Petersberg: Michael Imhof, 2012.

Hermand, Jost. *Geschichte der Germanistik*. Hamburg: Rowohlt, 1994.

Herzig, Arno. "1815–1933: Emanzipation und Akkulturation." *Jüdisches Leben in Deutschland*. Informationen zur politischen Bildung. Accessed December 19, 2021. https://www.bpb. de/shop/zeitschriften/izpb/7674/1815-1933-emanzipation-und-akkulturation/.

Heukäufer, Margarethe. *Und es gibt so wenig Menschen: Das kurze Leben des Künstlers Peter Kien*. Prague: Helena Osvaldová, 2009.

Holý, Jiří. "Tschechisch- und deutschsprachige Kultur in Theresienstadt." *Schnittstelle für Deutsche Sprache, Literatur und Kultur des mittleren und östlichen Europas* 2, no. 1 (2022): 41–56.

Hondius, Dienke. *Return. Holocaust Survivors and Dutch Anti-Semitism*. Translated by David Colmer. Westport: Praeger Publishers, 2003.

Horowitz, Sara. *Voicing the Void: Muteness and Memory in Holocaust Fiction*. Albany: SUNY Press, 1997.

Jaiser, Constanze. *Poetische Zeugnisse: Gedichte aus dem Frauen-Konzentrationslager Ravensbrück, 1939–1945*. Stuttgart: Metzler, 2000.

Jakob, Volker, and Annet van der Vort. *Anne Frank war nicht allein: Lebensgeschichten deutscher Juden in den Niederlanden*. Berlin: Dietz, 1988.

Jaskot, Paul. *The Architecture of Oppression: The SS, Forced Labor and the Nazi Monumental Building Economy*. London: Taylor & Francis Group, 1999.

Jenss, Harro, and Peter Reinicke, eds. *Der Arzt Hermann Strauß 1868–1944. Autobiographische Notizen und Aufzeichnungen aus dem Ghetto Theresienstadt*. Berlin: Hentrich & Hentrich, 2014.

Jeuck, Verona, and Werner Nostheide. *150 Jahre Pestalozzi-Verlag*. Erlangen: Pestalozzi-Verlag, 1994.

Jochem, Gerhard. "Biography of Frank A. Harris, Fürth." Accessed March 17, 2022. http://www.rijo.homepage.t-online.de/pdf/en_fu_ju_Harris_Frank.pdf.

Jewish Museum Berlin. "9 November 1938 / Kristallnacht." Accessed August 22, 2023. https://www.jmberlin.de/en/topic-9-november-1938.

Kolb, Bernhard. *Die Juden in Nürnberg 1839–1945*. Edited by Gerhard Jochem. Accessed February 6, 2022. http://www.rijo.homepage.t-online.de/pdf/DE_NU_JU_kolb_text.pdf.

Kaplan, Chaim. *Scroll of Agony. The Warsaw Diary of Chaim Kaplan*. Translated by Abraham I. Katsh. New York: Macmillan, 1965.

Kaplan, Marion A. *Der Mut zum Überleben. Jüdische Frauen und ihre Familien in Nazideutschland*. Translated by Christian Wiese. Berlin: Aufbau, 2001.

———. *Between Dignity and Despair: Jewish Life in Nazi Germany*. Oxford: Oxford University Press, 1998.

———. *Jüdisches Bürgertum: Frau, Familie und Identität im Kaiserreich*. Translated by Ingrid Strobl. Hamburg: Dölling und Galitz, 1991.

———. *The Making of the Jewish Middle Class. Women, Family, and Identity in Imperial Germany*. Oxford: Oxford University Press, 1991.

———. *Die jüdische Frauenbewegung in Deutschland. Organisation und Ziele des Jüdischen Frauenbundes 1904–1938*. Translated by Hainer Jober. Hamburg: Hans Christians, 1981.

Klein, Peter. "Theresienstadt: Ghetto oder Konzentrationslager?" In *Theresienstädter Studien und Dokumente*, edited by Jaroslava Milotová, Ulf Rathgeber, and Michael Wögerbauer, 28–35. Prague: Sefer, 2005.

Klüger, Ruth. *weiter leben. Eine Jugend*. München: dtv, 1994.

———. *Still Alive. A Holocaust Girlhood Remembered*. New York: Feminist Press, 2003.

Kohlhaas, Elisabeth. "Gertrud Slottke—Angestellte im niederländischen Judenreferat der Sicherheitspolizei." In *Karrieren der Gewalt. Nationalsozialistische Täterbiographien*, edited by Klaus-Michael Mallmann and Gerhard Paul, 207–218. Darmstadt: Wissenschaftliche Buchgesellschaft, 2004.

Kluxen, Andrea M., and Julia Krieger, eds. *Juden in Franken 1806 bis heute*. Würzburg: Ergon, 2011.

———. *Geschichte und Kultur der Juden in Nürnberg*. Würzburg: Ergon, 2014.

Kolářová, Eva. *Das Theresienstadt-Bild in Werken der Häftlinge*. Ustí nad Labem: albio international, 1998.

Lamberti, Marjorie. "Making Art in the Terezín Concentration Camp." *New England Review* 17, no. 4 (1995): 109–110.

Langlois, Gérard. "Histoire de la familie Löwensohn." 2009. Accessed April 20, 2022. http://www.rijo.homepage.t-online.de/pdf/FR_FU_JU_loewensohn.pdf.

Lavsky, Hagit Hadassa. *The Creation of the German-Jewish Diaspora. Interwar German-Jewish Immigration to Palestine, the USA, and England*. New York: Walter de Gruyter, 2017.

Löw, Andrea, Doris L. Bergen, and Anna Hájková, eds. *Alltag im Holocaust: Jüdisches Leben im Großdeutschen Reich 1941–1945*. Munich: Oldenbourg, 2013.

Mallmann, Klaus-Michael, and Gerhard Paul, eds. *Karrieren der Gewalt. Nationalsozialistische Täterbiographien*. Darmstadt: Wissenschaftliche Buchgesellschaft, 2004.

Manes, Philipp. *Als ob's ein Leben wär: Tatsachenbericht Theresienstadt 1942–1933*. Edited by Klaus Leist and Ben Barkow. Berlin: Ullstein, 2005.

———. *As If It were Life. A WWII Diary from the Theresienstadt Ghetto*. Edited by Klaus Leist and Ben Barkow. Translated by Janet Forster, Klaus Leist, and Ben Barkow. New York: Palgrave Macmillan, 2009.

McGlothlin, Erin. *Second-Generation Holocaust Literature: Legacies of Survival and Perpetration*. Rochester, NY: Camden House, 2006.

Mehring, Reinhard, ed. *Ethik nach Theresienstadt. Späte Texte des Prager Philosophen Emil Utitz*. Würzburg: Königshausen & Neumann, 2015.

Migdal, Ulrike, ed. *Und die Musik spielt dazu. Chansons und Satiren aus Theresienstadt*. Munich: Piper, 1986.

Milton, Sybil. "Art in the Context of Theresienstadt." In *Art, Music, Education as Strategies for Survival: Theresienstadt*, edited by Anne Dutlinger, 10–59. New York: Herodias, 2000.

Mintz, Alan. *Hurban. Responses to Catastrophe in Hebrew Literature*. Syracuse: Syracuse University Press, 1996.

Moll, Michael. *Lyrik in einer entmenschlichten Welt. Interpretationsversuche zu deutschsprachigen Gedichten aus nationalsozialistischen Gefängnissen, Ghettos und KZs*. Frankfurt: R. G. Fischer, 1988.

Moore, Bob. *Victims and Survivors. The Nazi Persecution of the Jews in the Netherlands*. New York: St. Martin's Press, 1997.

Müller, Arnd. *Geschichte der Juden in Nürnberg 1146–1945*. Nuremberg: Selbstverlag der Stadtbibliothek Nürnberg, 1968.

Nader, Andrés J. *Traumatic Verses: On Poetry from the Concentration Camps 1933–1945*. Rochester, NY: Camden House, 2007.

Peschel, Lisa, ed. *Performing Captivity, Performing Escape. Cabarets and Plays from the Terezín/Theresienstadt Ghetto*. London: Seagull Books, 2014.

———. "Das Theater in Theresienstadt und das Zweite Tschechische Kabarett: 'Geistiger Widerstand?'" In *Theresienstädter und Dokumente*, edited by Jaroslava Milotová and Anna Hájková, 84–114. Prague: Sefer, 2008.

Piper, Franciszek. "Blechhammer." Translated by Gerard Majka. In *The United States Holocaust Memorial Museum Encyclopedia of Ghettos and Camps: Early Camps, Youth Camps, Concentration Camps and Subcamps under the SS-Business Administration Office*, edited by Geoffrey P. Megargee, volume 1, part A, 227–228. Bloomington: Indiana University Press, 2009.

Presser, Jacques. *Ashes in the Wind. The Destruction of Dutch Jewry*. Translated by Arnold Pomerans. Detroit: Wayne State University Press, 1968.

Prestel, Claudia. "Frauenpolitik oder Parteipolitik? Jüdische Frauen in innerjüdischer Politik in der Weimarer Republik." *Archiv für Sozialgeschichte* 37 (1997): 121–155.

Raphael, Melissa. *Judaism and the Visual Image. A Jewish Theology of Art*. London: Bloomsbury, 2009.

Rittner, Carol, and John K. Roth, eds. *Different Voices: Women and the Holocaust*. New York: Paragon House, 1993.

Ritz, Christian. *Schreibtischtäter vor Gericht. Das Verfahren vor dem Münchener Landgericht wegen der Deportation der niederländischen Juden*. Paderborn: Ferdinand Schöningh, 2012.

Roos, Daniel. *Julius Streicher und "Der Stürmer" 1923–1945*. Paderborn: Ferdinand Schöningh, 2014.

Rosenberg, Leibl. *Spuren und Fragmente. Jüdische Bücher, Jüdische Schicksale in Nürnberg*. Nuremberg: Israelitische Kultusgemeinde und die Stadt Nürnberg, 2000.

———. *Im Schatten der Burg: Jüdisches Leben in Nürnberg*. Nuremberg: Israelitische Kultusgemeinde, 2019.

Roskies, David. *Against the Apocalypse. Responses to Catastrophe in Modern Jewish Culture*. Cambridge, MA: Harvard University Press, 1984.

Ross, Steven J., Wolf Gruner, and Lisa Ansell, eds. *New Perspectives on Kristallnacht: After 80 Years, the Nazi Pogrom in Global Comparison*. West Lafayette: Purdue University Press, 2019.

Roth, John K. *The Failure of Ethics: Confronting the Holocaust, Genocide, and Other Mass Atrocities*. Oxford: Oxford University Press, 2015.

Rothkirchen, Livia. *The Jews of Bohemia and Moravia. Facing the Holocaust*. Lincoln: University of Nebraska Press, 2005.

Rovit, Rebecca, and Alvin Goldfarb, eds. *Theatrical Performances during the Holocaust: Texts, Documents, Memoirs*. Baltimore: Johns Hopkins University Press, 1999.

Rowland, Antony. *Poetry as Testimony. Witnessing and Memory in Twentieth-Century Poems*. Hoboken: Taylor & Francis, 2014.

———. *Holocaust Poetry: Awkward Poetics in the Work of Sylvia Plath, Geoffrey Hill, Tony Harrison and Ted Hughes*. Edinburgh: Edinburgh University Press, 2005.

Schaumann, Caroline. *Memory Matters: Generational Responses to Germany's Nazi Past in Recent Women's Literature*. Berlin: De Gruyter, 2008.

Schmidt, Alexander. "Scheinbare Normalität: Drei Skizzen zur Geschichte der Nürnberger Juden 1918 bis 1938." In *Geschichte und Kultur der Juden in Nürnberg*, edited by Andrea M. Kluxen and Julia Krieger, 285–313. Würzburg: Ergon, 2014.

Schwertfeger, Ruth. *Women in Theresienstadt. Voices from a Concentration Camp.* Oxford: Berg, 1988.

Seiderer, Georg. "Entwicklungslinien jüdischer Geschichte in Nürnberg von der Wiederansiedlung bis zur Weimarer Republik. In *Geschichte und Kultur der Juden in Nürnberg,* edited by Andrea M. Klusen and Julia Krieger, 165–179. Würzburg: Ergon, 2014.

Spender, Stephen. "Introduction." In Abba Kovner and Nelly Sachs, *Selected Poems.* Translated by Shirley Kaufman and Nurit Orchan, 7–18. Harmondsworth: Penguin, 1971.

Spies, Gerty. *Drei Jahre Theresienstadt.* Munich: Kaiser, 1984.

———. *Three Years in Theresienstadt. How One Woman Survived the Holocaust.* Translated by Jutta R. Tragnitz. Amherst, NY: Prometheus Books, 1997.

The Nuremberg Municipal Museums. *Documentation Center Nazi Party Rally Grounds.* Accessed May 19, 2022. https://museums.nuernberg.de/documentation-center/the-site/the-nazi-party-rally-grounds/information-system-rally-grounds/point-08.

Young, James E. *Beschreiben des Holocaust. Darstellung und Folgen der Interpretation.* Translated by Christa Schuenke. Frankfurt: Suhrkamp, 1997.

———. *Writing and Rewriting the Holocaust: Narrative and the Consequences of Interpretation.* Bloomington: Indiana University Press, 1988.

Václavek, Ludvík. "Zur Problematik der deutschen Lyrik aus Theresienstadt." In *Theresienstädter Studien und Dokumente,* edited by Miroslav Kárný, Raimund Kemper, and Margita Kárná, 128–134. Prague: Sefer, 1994.

Wager, Melanie. "Warenhausjude, Wäschejude, Autojude. *Der Stürmer* und die Arisierung." In *Entrechtet. Entwürdigt. Beraubt. Die Arisierung in Nürnberg und Fürth,* edited by Matthias Henkel and Eckart Dietzfelbinger, 17–39. Petersberg: Michael Imhof, 2012.

Weber, Reinhard. "Berufliche Ausgrenzung von jüdischen Rechtsanwälten und Justizbediensteten." In *Entrechtet. Entwürdigt. Beraubt. Die Arisierung in Nürnberg und Fürth,* edited by Matthias Henkel and Eckart Dietzfelbinger, 83–89. Petersberg: Michael Imhof, 2012.

———. *Das Schickal der jüdischen Rechtsanwälte in Bayern nach 1933.* Munich: Oldenbourg, 2006.

Weber, Ilse. *In deinen Mauern wohnt das Leid. Gedichte aus dem KZ Theresienstadt.* Gerlingen: Bleicher, 1991.

Wolff, Lynn ed. *A Modernist in Exile. The International Reception of H. G. Adler (1910–1988).* Oxford: Legenda, 2019.

Wlodarski, Amy Lynn. "Musical Testimonies of Terezín and the Possibilities of Contrapuntal Listening." *Music & Politics* 16, no. 2 (2022): 1–21. Accessed October 21, 2022.

———. *Musical Witness and Holocaust Representation.* Cambridge: Cambridge University Press, 2015.

———. "The Testimonial Aesthetics of Different Trains." *Journal of the American Musicology Society* 63, no. 1 (2010): 99–141.

Wontschik, Ilka. "*Es war wohl ein anderer Stern, auf dem wir lebten.*" *Künstlerinnen in Theresienstadt.* Berlin: Hentrich & Hentrich, 2014.

Yad Vashem. Deportation Records. Accessed November 2, 2022. https://deportation.yad-vashem.org/index.html?language=en&itemId=5092551.

Ziegler, Sandra. *Gedächtnis und Identität der KZ-Erfahrung. Niederländische und deutsche Augenzeugenberichte des Holocaust.* Würzburg: Königshausen & Neumann, 2006.

Archives Consulted

Family Archives

Personal archive Thomas Runkel, Germany.
Personal archive Henk Haas, Netherlands.
Personal archive George Rogers, United Kingdom.

Public Archives

Netherlands

Nederlands Instituut voor Oorlogsdocumentatie (NIOD), Amsterdam, Netherlands

Kampen en gevangenissen buiten Nederland, 4.1 Kampleven, 90–1190 Verklaringen van voormalig gevangenen over hun wedervaren, NIOD, 250d, 501 Else Dormitzer.

Proces E. Rajakowitsch, "Verhoren-II." Verklaringen von S. J. Flörsheim, R. T. Haas, H. A. Ph. Hartog, D. Schäffer, G. Wijsmuller-Meijer, B. Zwaaf en M. Zwaaf, 1963–1965, 270d, 1.3.

Germany

Stadtarchiv Nürnberg / City Archives, Nuremberg.

Nürnberger Israelitisches Gemeindeblatt / Nürnberger Fürther Israelitisches Gemeindeblatt / Nürnberger Israelitisches Gemeindeblatt, Jahrgang 1921–1938.

Meldekarte Else Dormitzer, C21/X, Nr.2_263.

United Kingdom

Wiener Holocaust Library, London, Great Britain

Korrespondenz mit den CV-Landesverbänden betr. propagandistische Tätigkeit von Else Dormitzer in den CV-Landesverbänden, 289 Blätter, 1920–31, 55/39/1608.

Eyewitness Account Else Dormitzer, "Experiences in Nuremberg, Holland, Theresienstadt, and during the Transport back to Holland," P.III.h. (Theresienstadt), no. 41.

Eyewitness Account Else Dormitzer, "Life in Theresienstadt," P.III.h. (Theresienstadt), no. 560.
Eyewitness Account Else Dormitzer, "The Night of Broken Glass," P.ii.d.no.37.
Correspondence with Else Dormitzer, 26 May 1952–3 October 1958, 3000/9/1/347.

Israel

Yad Vashem, Jerusalem

Else Dormitzer, 0.2–53, 0.2.–139, 0.2–392 (Wiener Holocaust Library Collection).

Images

Stadtarchiv Nürnberg / City Archives, Nuremberg, Germany

A 38 Nr. F50-10; A 47 Nr. 24-6; A 47 Nr. KS 24-7

Private photographs and documents

Personal archive Thomas Runkel
Personal archive Henk Haas

Index

Printed in the USA
CPSIA information can be obtained
at www.ICGtesting.com
JSHW081402010724
65696JS00005B/233